Nothing else is like these pieces. There is a certain dream character to them, as when we recognize everyone in the room, except that they are different. As in a transforming mythography, they are the same and not-same. It's a singular work, an evolved form of memoiristic writing.
—Michael Palmer

Quite something to pull off the explication of such complex ideas in the guise of narrative, character and a fair share of belly laughs.
—Amei Wallach

The poet's job, Rosenberg cautions, is nothing less than to foretell the species' next move.
—Jack Kimball
Poetry Project Newsletter

SEE WHAT YOU THINK

Critical Essays for the Next Avant Garde

David Rosenberg

SPUYTENDUYVIL

© 2002, 2003 David Rosenberg
ISBN 1-881471-88-8
LCCN 2002114150

Spuyten Duyvil
PO Box 1852
Cathedral Station
NYC 10025
1-800-886-5304
http://spuytenduyvil.net

9 8 6 5 4 3 2 1

ACKNOWLEDGMENTS AND DEDICATION

"The Prophetic Poet of the Twentieth Century" first appeared in *Open Letter: A Journal of Poetics and Theory* (London, Canada) edited by Frank Davey. The initial responses of Harold Bloom, David Shapiro and Tod Thilleman were inspirational. John Ashbery's letters kept me awake. I could not imagine writing a page of this book, nor the work that continues, without the gorgeous sensibility of Rhonda Rosenberg awaiting it, my co-author and to whom this book is dedicated.

Contents

frontispiece   9

Group-portrait in a Vermont Kitchen   13

The Classics   33

The Prophetic Poet of the Twentieth Century   53

The Future of Visionary Poetry   93

frontispiece

These pieces are about history, a cultural history worn down to the natural history supporting it. I think of James Schuyler and the great Canadian poet, bpNichol, as being still alive. What will they write next is answered by the new resonance of their work at the frontiers of ecological and evolutionary science. To put it another way, they are scientists today, and their work explores—sees—along the direct line between childhood and the childhood of Homo sapiens. I would call that line ecological thought, or post-Holocaust, in which the death of the organism and the extinction of the species are felt as one. We are alive to read Jimmy and Barrie now, but imagine what the work looks like when Homo sapiens becomes extinct, as we surely will. That is what they saw, a time apart from time that could only be natural—and that could be thought of as unearthed a hundred thousand years ago.

—April, 2003, near the Everglades

The seconds of torment of Mohammed Dura's death were appropriated as 'a spectacle,' broadcast over and over on French television, outside any context, without checking the source of the shooting, and affirming Israeli responsibility for a deliberate attack (which was later proved to be a lie). A poem composed in his memory by the Palestinian poet, Mahmoud Darwish, appropriates expressions from the classic poem by the national Hebrew poet Bialik, "On the Slaughter," which was composed in response to the Kishinev pogrom. The Hebrew translation of the Darwish poem, which appeared immediately and without any criticism in the literary supplement of *Haaretz*, was an expression of the ideological appropriation of death and the internalization of mythic violence out of an identification with the 'Other'— and a rejection of the 'I' and its story.

—Michal Govrin

Martyrs or Survivors? Thoughts on the Mythical Dimension of the Story War

He has that strange quality of an earth that one has never seen and of things destroyed as they have never been destroyed.

—Gertrude Stein

Picasso

GROUP-PORTRAIT IN A VERMONT KITCHEN

For several months in 1973 I lived in the guest apartment of poet Kenward Elmslie's house in Greenwich Village. Independence resided in my used, rusty-red Plymouth. One Friday in early spring Kenward asked if I would like to drive him, his dog Whippoorwill, and artist-poet Joe Brainard to his summer house in Vermont. Along the way we picked up the poets John Ashbery and James Schuyler.

Among this group, youthful Joe held his ground by seeming to have more important things on his mind, things that applied to his work. When he wasn't working, Joe's anxiety-level was one step away from the persona of a Russian intellectual, exiled to Siberia with no pencils. And—no paper, scissors, paste or brushes for thousands of miles. Why bother shouting? What was there worth saying anything about? These were the questions reflected on Joe's face while he hung about before dinner as the others held forth in the kitchen.

In general, Joe didn't talk alot. He often scanned the floor, as if he had dropped something. But when it came to art, Joe's visual and hearing senses seemed spread evenly and thoroughly throughout the surface of his skin, a tiny, infinitesimal seeing and receiving nodule located within each cell, rendering his prominent ears and glasses moot.

Kenward was chief cook and Jimmy was chief prosecutor, questioning the cook desultorily about what went into things and when things would be ready to eat. Recovering from a recent hospitalization and not walking much, Jimmy was the house Buddha, to whose ultimate approval everything had to be submitted, including the weather. And this included last night's, this morning's, tomorrow's, this afternoon's, the actual version and the newspaper or radio's version. Cooking ingredients were described to Jimmy as if they were newly discovered wildflowers in the grass driveway and as if he was a housecat. Color, smell, texture, etc. John, chief assistant for everything, was also curious, though less so, padding from kitchen to living room and back in a broad valentine apron.

That weekend, however, John announced he was composing a longish poem about the Kennedy assassination. Mystery was its genre, chosen to secretly echo the "Mystery Page" of the monthly magazine, "Vermont Sewing Circle," of which there were several issues to be seen around the house. The current one, folded open to the page in question, was entitled "A Lost Soul." John then informed us that the opening of the poem revolved around JFK's moment of dying and when or whether the soul departed. A heated discussion about the Zapruder film followed, with Jimmy noting that certain frames showed "the life going out of him."

"That's a euphemism," John queried, "for the medieval concept of the soul departing, isn't it?"

"You're the expert on religion," Kenward said without looking at me, tossing parsley in the soup, an item he had previously instructed us should be added sooner rather than later. "What about the soul, Rosey?" Another nickname at the time was "perfesser," though I held only an adjunct post at a Long Island college. However, none of the others had set foot for years in an institution of higher learning, or what Jimmy referred to as "the lead box".

"The soul is rendered in the eyes," I answered. "You can see JFK closing his eyes as he is hit in the Zapruder film, though I don't remember if he opened them again."

> "But how far can it swim out through the eyes
> And still return safely to its nest?"

These were the lines John could be seen trying out to himself under his breath. He then repeated them aloud.

Kenward, arbiter of each word, weighed them in his mind as he did each single asparagus stalk he was lining up on an appetizer plate, followed by a drizzle of mustard. For each line John uttered, Kenward would nod his head or occasionally say no. A "no" might have the force of a snapped window shade on John, and he would repeat the line, this time with a different word or intonation, often enunciating it in brackets with an invisible questionmark. This time it was a nod and in the silence that followed Jimmy commented in verse while John scrambled to write it down, as if it would never be repeated. If you weren't paying strict attention as John was, you might think Jimmy a hypochondriac, dutifully reciting the doctor's instructions.

> "The soul has to stay where it is,
> Even though restless, hearing raindrops at the pane,
> The sighing of autumn leaves thrashed by the wind,
> Longing to be free, outside, but it must stay
> Posing in this place. It must move
> As little as possible—"

John stopped him. "Is that a line-break after 'place' or 'move'?" he asked.

"I see it all as prose," answered Jimmy, "but with virgules. So put a virgule after 'move,' to balance the one after 'stay'."

John muttered Jimmy's answer as he rewrote the words in verse form. "I don't like virgules," he snorted softly.

"Besides, you lose the harmonic resonance with the previous line, which ends with 'wind'," added Kenward, still the top lyricist, now peering over John's shoulder at the writing, big salad mixing bowl in hand.

"Wait," said Joe. "The soul is not a soul." We were all stopped in our tracks. Then John burst out laughing, and in a mock-heroic response, cried: "The pity of it smarts, makes hot tears spurt."

At times like these, Joe was the down to earth one. In the kitchen, he would be shucker of peas, slicer of tomatoes, grinder of peppercorns, the breader and the wine smeller. It was all quite remarkable, considering his body seemed about to fall to pieces, the legs entangled, arms akimbo, his head rolling from his neck. It was the body language of a new kind of music, portents of the future.

They might start atonally, but when they came out, Joe's lines achieved the simplicity of the word "Vermont" uttered beside a small green mountain. When John asked if it was just too much to at least "imagine" that there was a soul—a soul in quotes—

Joe put his left hand up, as if asking for permission to think a moment, and then stammered "I mean," repeating it several times before the words dove forward, like a swimmer into the eye of the pool:

> "That the soul is not a soul,
> Has no secret, is small, and it fits
> Its hollow perfectly: its room, our moment of attention."

Again, silence enveloped us in an end-quote. John started beating on the table with his tablespoon. "So where is JFK now? You want to concentrate on Oswald: the eye gazing through the crosshairs as the rifle-sight holds the president's life in a momentary round ball."

"Ashes, don't be a nincompoop," Jimmy growled. "Pull back from the glass and you've got a scene with thousands lining the street, chasing the car, reporting the event on radio and TV." Jimmy seemed to have thought about the poem before John had begun it. "Think back to how many voices we ourselves heard on 'The day we saw what nobody will forget,' Cronkite crooning that into the yawn box."

"And forget the eyes," Jimmy almost hissed. He asked us to think about the soundtrack to that day, to think of the voices as they

> "Uttered light or dark speech that became part of you
> Like light behind windblown fog and sand,

> Filtered and influenced by it, until no part
> Remains that is surely you. Those voices in the dusk
> Have told you all and still the tale goes on
> In the form of memories deposited in irregular
> Clumps of crystals—"

—"Whoa!" John shouted. "Any more and you'll be claiming this is a collaboration!" John started hitting Jimmy on the head lightly with his spoon, as if cracking a hardboiled egg.

Kenward plopped the big wooden salad bowl of overflowing greens on the kitchen table in front of John. "Now Johnny-boy," he said, "we all know you're the major poet. None of us could have thought up 'The Double Dream of Spring' and received all those double-length reviews."

"That's it!" exclaimed John. "It's more like a dream." He further explained that a dream was larger in scope than any scene or story, that it took in sights and sounds, people and places, and tied them into a deeper conspiracy of sources, a never-ending conspiracy...

> "What should be the vacuum of a dream
> Becomes continually replete as the source of dreams
> Is being tapped so that this one dream
> May wax, flourish like a cabbage rose,
> Defying sumptuary laws, leaving us
> To awake and try to begin living in what
> Has now become a slum."

John reached for a clump of lettuce and began to munch. The rest of us were shaking our heads, as if John's words were water in our ears. Here we were, putting in our two cents worth but John comes along and takes it to another level. Of course that's what was needed, the largeness of myth that only a dream could replicate. It had all felt like a dream to begin with. None of us could deny that Kennedy was dead, none could speculate that he was hiding out in Argentina while undergoing plastic surgery. The assassin himself could still be anywhere among us, more palpable than a hovering soul—the death of Oswald had foreclosed the chance to discover who might have been his accomplices.

"The man behind the green knoll, for instance," I concluded, after voicing the preceding. Jimmy snickered, but John spun it out, without hesitation:

> "Why be unhappy with this arrangement, since
> Dreams prolong us as they are absorbed?
> Something like living occurs, a movement
> Out of the dream into its codification."

So that is why JFK is still with us, John seemed to explain. His murder prolonged a dream that began that fateful day. The dream—not the death and aftermath—is the mystery in this narrative. We are still in it, our hearts drumming in everyday pursuit. We cannot have an after until the story is solved. This awareness dawned on the rest of us almost in unison, like a true dawn. And "John" echoed "John," we grasped in disbelief. The spooky repetition confirmed his sinecure: we were into something beyond a lyric afterlife.

Kenward went to the window, opened it, and pulled from the outside sill a potted plant. "A breath of fresh air would be nice," he said. He brought the plant to the table and began pinching off leaves, crumbling them between thumb and forefinger, sprinkling the contents over the salad, and suggesting the following lines, "to acknowledge the canonicity of JFK." Like half-mad Hamlet telling Ophelia of his father, he added "His death is with us still..."—in the platitudinous tone of Polonius, that she would be sure to miss the irony of, unconsciously locked in rebellion to her father's will. But this note of portentousness was Kenward's signature. He liked to pull intellectual rank, so long as it remained among present company, quoting from the Western canon as if we were about to dismiss it. Continuing in the guise of Polonius, he intoned

> "The moment takes such a big bite out of the haze
> Of pleasant intuition it comes after.
> The locking into place is "death itself,"
> As Berg said of a phrase in Mahler's Ninth;
> Or, to quote Imogen in Cymbeline, "There cannot
> Be a pinch in death more sharp than this,' for,
> Though only exercise or tactic, it carries
> The momentum of a conviction that had been building."

There it was. The death of JFK had become canonical, an idealized loss of king—of father, son or brother—and it now pinches us, crimps our possibility to imagine new selves. We must remain locked in a Western dream-canon without hope of an afterlife. And here we stay (exactly who we were on that critical day) to be pinched awake precisely at that moment we are convinced we've been locked into place: each of us a buried corpse sealed in the earth.

Allow me to digress on the point of "exercise" Kenward had added. In tennis, point after point, he would return my rarely brilliant, lunging, more often rash shot down the line as calmly as if he were reading a newspaper, returning it cross-court to a spot in-bounds I had not previously known existed. I uttered oath after oath on the court; finally, there were no words for this embarrassment, just a kind of afterlife in which language did not exist.

"After all the post-everythings, at last we may confront JFK in heaven," continued the opera-minded Kenward, foreshadowing "Angels in America," "and you, Joe, have already been drawing it on the porch."

"You mean," stuttered Joe,

> "What is this universe the porch of
> As it veers in and out, back and forth,
> Refusing to surround us and still the only
> Thing we can see?"

The lines tripped off Joe's tongue, but hesitantly. "I know," chimed John. "We were all Marilyns in love with him. Who would kill the desire of the goddess but a man so blinded by love he forgot about heaven? Who knows what Shakespearean mixup might occur there." John closed his eyes, holding an imaginary lute to his breast, plucking it soundly in accompaniment:

> "Love once
> Tipped the scales but now is shadowed, invisible,
> Though mysteriously present, around somewhere,
> But we know it cannot be sandwiched
> Between two adjacent moments."

Whether this was JFK's or Oswald's heaven was unclear. Yet it was the conviction of everyone present in the kitchen that hazy Vermont late afternoon that we had to get to the bottom of this dream to determine how the guilt had been apportioned. For it was clear we were all implicated—Marilyn had made that clear. The very day was a dream, moving from measure to measure, with Joe's hand measuring light and shadow onto paper (he was sketching us now); Kenward keeping time with wooden salad spoon baton; John pluck-plucking in his valentine apron while writing everything down with the other hand; me taking notes in my head like the court fool, and

Jimmy insisting with pounding fist that the measure was the murder weapon, that it shot us back into

> "our dreaming, as we had never thought
> it would end, in worn daylight with the painted
> Promise showing through as a gage, a bond.
> This nondescript, never-to-be defined daytime is
> The secret of where it takes place
> And we can no longer return to the various
> Conflicting statements gathered, lapses of memory
> Of the principal witnesses."

Jimmy's resemblance to Raymond Burr was striking. We all knew what "it" was now, we all knew the "it" we had partially murdered, for we had all knitted our own ballerina, until "getting her foot right" was more important than life itself. On point, supporting her (I forget exactly how the ballet tropes entered) we could no longer return to being merely alive, disheveled in a chair, watching as if from behind the camera.

Just that afternoon I had tried it out once more, snapping pictures from the broken window in the writing cabin some distance behind Kenward's house. It was a place none had spoken of, and I had stumbled upon it while looking for nature friezes in the woods. A "No Trespassing" sign had broken the spell of looking, and before I could decide if the sign meant me I spotted the ramshackle one-room hut, plunged in. The table was withered, the chair so rickety a ghost would have snapped it. Jimmy worked here some years back, I recalled, and the forest had recovered it's privileged position, in the same slow but inexorable way that Jimmy would eventually win the Pulitzer Prize and poetry might one day reclaim its wildness. I am looking forward to look back, though, which is what Jimmy had counseled against. We must stick to ground zero, he insisted, in order to catch the attentive Oswald in the wild instant that had rocked us to sleep.

Far from denying Marilyn her desire and thus gaining her attention, Lee finds himself but an accessory—peripheral as a poet—in the larger mystery. Does he own the dream? Is there a heaven where Marilyn can lock him in her gaze? Perhaps he has already been forgotten, ploughed under like an academic poet, and all is now focussed upon where the dream came from and if JFK had authored it. These questions I read aloud to the group from the notes I'd been deputized to take while John was on a bathroom break.

"He who had pulled the trigger could be deprived of authorship as bodily as the Yahwist had been airbrushed from God's presence," I concluded, nodding toward Joe's brushes airing out on the kitchen floor. For abstruse reasons (at the obvious places he could be emotionless) John began laughing and would not stop, brandishing a pail and torturing us like the

Dutch Cleanser woman, insisting the floor was not clean enough to set Joe's hallowed brushes upon. Although we did not completely get John's joke, his infectious laughs had us all clutching our ribs and gasping for air between guffaws. Whipoorwill the dog was also beside himself, jumping into the laps of each one of us in turn, desperate and comical.

When John calmed down he stared at me and repeated, "He who had pulled the trigger—the poet of our lives—is not to blame?"

"No," I answered, still reading from the notes,

> "He blames himself (though
> Secretly satisfied with the result), imagining
> He had a say in the matter and exercised
> An option of which he was hardly conscious,
> Unaware that necessity circumvents such resolutions
> So as to create something new
> For itself, that there is no other way,
> That the history of creation proceeds according to
> Stringent laws, and that things
> Do get done in this way, but never the things
> We set out to accomplish and wanted so desperately
> To see come into being."

I thought these lines sounded slack, but John recopied them like all the others into one of those marbelized black-and-white covered—timeless—cheap schoolboy notebooks. So Oswald was not really in the picture—not, after all, a witness to the drama unfolding on the as yet black-and-white of the day's TV. Joe was picking up the now self-conscious brushes. This act struck the rest of us around the table as the most incongruous of any yet imagined. If it were Lee Harvey Oswald and he was bending to pick up his rifles and retreat to his room in embarrassment, it would make more sense.

After all, Joe was the one among us who transcended poetry, the one who painted and pasted into life the daily implements of all our wishes for immortality—right down to the knives and forks, the pencils and notebooks. He could have caught Lee best. When he turned to go, brushes in hand, it occurred to us simultaneously that we were the assembled party and that he was the detective, ready to reveal the genre's final culprit. Brush in hand, we imagined him reconstructing the scene:

> "There is room for one bullet in the chamber:
> Our looking through the wrong end
> Of the telescope as you fall back at a speed
> Faster than that of light to flatten ultimately
> Among the features of the room."

Were we in the room reflected in the picture-tube eye of 1963—or rather, in the Vermont group portrait Joe was later to paint? For that is how it was done, inconspicuous as sheep grazing in Vermont, his work completed before the eye could decide what to focus upon. Apparently lounging around without an idea in his head, suddenly the next day there would be a museumful of finished works: drawings, collages, paintings, and poems too. In this case, we were sketched in a group portrait. When that portrait was painted (permit me to look forward to look back) we would recognize it as the smoking-gun residue of a dream flattened.

The strange thing concerning memory is that I can't remember what we ate after the salad, not a shred of smell or taste, as if I didn't eat at all nor did any of the others. Food became words, as natural as what lay outside the windows, in the ground, on the trees, in the air. There were indoor artifacts that were exquisite reminders of the food—like plastic replicas of sushi in restaurant windows: pinecones, dried flowers, except they were not manmade but instead made by... whom? Nature was landlord of this place, and at certain times she even dictated we had to vacate for an hour, to stroll down the dirt road to the highway.

She wanted some wildness in our heads also, some insistent en masse cricket-chirping of the synapses. All this continued after dinner each day when, lubricated by the evening meal, we'd go to our rickety standing-lamp work corners, leaving Kenward to do the dishes. He never touched them. Rather, they were there in the sink in the morning and we all did them together, though John, in his big valentine apron again, would slip over to the dining table, fetch the "Vermont Sewing Circle," and begin reading aloud to us as we worked:

> "Has anyone knitted a pumpkin pie? Unusual as it sounds, my sister Ida specialized in pies, especially cherry ones with the criss-cross pastry crust burnt black-brown on top, like an outdoor grill, and the cherry filling red as coals glowing within..."

The night we stayed around the table for John's poem was different, though, to be memorialized in the group painting Joe would make from his sketch. But first, summer would turn into autumn, then winter, and when spring rolled around again the poem did too, in print.

The first surprise upon reading the finished poem in "The New Yorker" was that it opened with what we all agreed were to be the last lines: the assassination unfolding on TV. That way, we, the assembled in the kitchen, would become transformed into witness and jury of the monstrous outlaw. For us, in that time and place, there was no more common eye around us than the eye of the insect, outnumbering our own by the hundreds of thousands, all within earshot of that house in Vermont, and in particular the crickets playing their endless raga outside the human dream.

Instead of opening out to this in the end, as we'd intended, John puzzled us when we first encountered the poem in magazine form. He had turned the TV in 1963 into the common bugeye through which we humans, in our own hundreds of thousands that mythical day of our dream, peered.

> "We have seen the city; it is the gibbous
> Mirrored eye of an insect. All things happen
> On its balcony and are resumed within,
> But the action is the cold, syrupy flow
> Of a Pageant. One feels too confined,
> Sifting the April sunlight for clues,
> In the mere stillness of the ease of its
> Parameter."

Where we had ended the poem, John opened it—in Washington, D.C., the funereal march through the streets, everything moving in the same slow-motion of the Zapruder film, allowing us to glimpse the bullet as it exited JFK's temple.

And then, what to make of the poem's newly-fabricated title, "Self-portrait in a Convex Mirror?" Framed oval mirrors in Kenward's house there were, yet nothing you would construe as convex. Furthermore, John had made such a point of including all our suggestions that it should have remained what we originally called it, "Group-portrait in a Vermont Kitchen." When Joe's painting was exhibited many years later, that was the title he retained.

Finally, why did John veil the murders of JFK and Oswald, rendering them so subtle that readers might miss them? It didn't take long, however, to realize how heavy a burden was hung on him. Were he thought to have punctured the dream while most poets were still testing the boundaries, he would have been vilified like Rimbaud after "Illuminations." Instead, prizes, including the Pulitzer, were lavished on our poem-in-disguise, in John's name, and shorn of its disturbing subject it was hailed as the pivotal work of the second half of the century. We all went to the congratulatory parties, however, strangely warm toward John in our feelings.

Memory must remain mysterious, since without it the past would exist only in pictures, or artifacts. Nevertheless, what grows stronger in memory with each passing year is Joe's original sketching of us which later became the portrait. It was like the bullet in our national dream, dispersing all words, so that I remember Joe—Joe himself, on that night—above all. The images of Joe, uncertain of what was to come next, brushes on the floor—smiling, raising his hand, or bending forward in concentration as he sketched—stand in for actual memory, as it flattens into day. And because he is no longer here, brought down too young by the Age, I'm condemned to reconstruct the crime, in order to hear again the dream of being poets together.

The Classics

I was often a guest at the graduate poetry seminars of Harold Bloom at New York University in the late nineteen-eighties. During this period, Bloom and I were completing *The Book of J*, a collaboration to be published in 1990, and I was pumped up for the big leagues. One day in the spring of '89, John Ashbery was invited to attend the class that would be discussing his recent provocative poem, "Girls on the Classics." This powerful work, several pages in length, had brought the blood of the feminist movement to a boil—in particular, a literary wing that the New York Times described as "an increasingly borderless lesbian rock and poetry scene."

Ten years later, in 1999, Farrar, Straus and Giroux published a book-length expansion of the poem, now entitled *Girls on the Run*, in which Ashbery finally responded to the biting criticism he had received, including such cruel and unfair remarks as "[Ashbery] couldn't tell a girl from a fork in the road." In the earlier decade, therefore, considerable effort had been expended to avoid these low-minded detractors by keeping the class a secret. An erroneous date had been put out, corrected only the preceding week, to throw the uninvited lesbians off.

So I was surprised to find the normally half-empty classroom filled to the rafters with students. The news had leaked out around campus yet apparently no further, for no lesbians were to be seen (in those revolutionary days, the artistic-minded ones stood out in whitish lipstick, blackened crewcuts, and red, high-heeled faux workboots). I was seated in the side front row between my friends, the poet David Shapiro, who had written the first critical study of Ashbery, and the Israeli poet Michal Govrin, who had been invited to the following week's seminar, when Allen Ginsberg's *Kaddish* would be the subject, but who had been confused by the shell game of changing dates. Ashbery peeked in the door before Bloom arrived, and walked up to me with a surprising "Hi David," as if he had come expressly to visit me. Shy about entering any further, he might have stood frozen there had not an attentive student brought a folding chair down from the upper levels of the classroom's stadium seating and placed it to one side of the lectern.

At last, Bloom made his customary late entry, closing the door behind him with an always bewildering delicacy. No student dared to come later than this, to suffer Bloom's studied glare, followed by a comment in mock-sympathy, such as "I trust no tragedy has preceded this base intrusion." One week, a student had actually countered, "My girlfriend drove into a stop sign." Bloom had hardly begun to speak, in fact, when the door was loudly pushed open and Allen Ginsberg came in, strode right up to Bloom at the lectern, put his hands together in prayerful Buddhist supplication, and said, more to the audience than to Bloom, "Forgive my belatedness, Professor Bloom, and allow me to sit at your feet."

Upon which Allen folded his legs in a meditative pose on the floor directly facing Bloom's lectern, gazing up at him like a rapt student. A titter made its way around the large room as Bloom, quickly sizing up Allen's error, explained that it was not Ginsberg's fault and was rather an embarrassment of riches to have poets so "different" as Ashbery and Ginsberg together. Now it was Allen's turn to appear stunned, noticing at last John Ashbery shifting uncomfortably in the seat adjacent to the lectern.

"Different?" Allen repeated in his broad basso voice. A hush came over the room. "How, different?"

"Allow me to continue, Mr. Ginsberg," Bloom piped louder, "and perhaps I can explain that. Excuse us as well for this mystification of dates. As the students have not yet read your poem, we will take up

Kaddish next week, though I will allude to it, if I may."

"We've read it, we've read it," came a raft of spontaneous outbursts from the students. Pretending not to hear, Bloom began to read from the beginning of "Girls on the Classics":

> Our fashions are in fashion
> Only briefly, then they go out
> And stay that way for a long time. Then they come back in
> For a while. Then, in maybe a million years, they go out of
>   fashion
> And stay there.

"Putting this visionary statement in the mouth of a girl," trumpeted Bloom, "Mr. Ashbery shows how a revisionist poetics turns time upside down. It may be unlikely that a young girl would be old enough to have experience of changing and returning fashions, but it is certainly impossible that she would have thought beyond human history and in terms of evolutionary theory, which an eon of 'a million years' suggests."

Glancing sidelong, I noticed that John was looking down at his shoes, as if he had already fallen behind Bloom's exegesis.

"Visionary?" gently boomed Allen Ginsberg. "I beg to differ. "'Visionary' is a spiritual trip involving an alteration of perception, a basic turning about at the root of consciousness—changing the texture of consciousness."

Bloom did not like being turned from the role of lecturer into one of moderator. "Please, Mr. Ginsberg," he huffed, "please allow me to establish the context with which my students are familiar. The word 'visionary' has been elaborated in earlier classes from a work by William Blake, 'The Mental Traveler.' Blake's vision about the education of a girl is the ground upon which Mr. Ashbery's poem seems to me to rest. Both make a shambles of ordinary time by showing that the apparent single-mindedness of youth is overturned by the inner sense of time a young girl acquires with the onset of menstruation. The pull of the moon has frustrated the all-seeing sun, so to speak, and I repeat, the duration of time is turned upside down."

"No 'ordinary' time, all 'visionary' time," Allen commented in a lowered voice, as if to himself, though nobody missed hearing it.

"Let's allow Mr. Ashbery to be heard on it," Bloom hurriedly continued.

> …the concept of duration, which kills
> Surely as a serpent hiding behind a stump.
> Our phrase books began to feel useless—for once
> You have learned a language, what is there to do but forget it?

"For Mr. Ashbery, vision expands beyond the human, the human time of language—occluded by the moon, so to speak." Bloom waved his arm toward the ceiling, though it was two in the afternoon and the sun shone brightly. "Our notion of time is bound by culture, suggests Mr. Ashbery (notice the myth-making we talked about last week) and once the sexual serpent appears it's time to forget the girl's prior innocence."

A slight smirk emerged on John's lips, barely noticeable. But it was Allen who responded, quoting from "The Mental Traveler" while Bloom shuffled his notes.

> Till he becomes a bleeding youth
> And she becomes a Virgin bright
> Then he rends up his Manacles
> And binds her down for his delight

In a professorial tone, Allen added: "Turned upside down is right. But why reduce its wildness and call it an allegory of sun and moon?"

"No, no," countered Bloom, "not a reduction but rather an enlargement, an—"

Bloom was stopped in his tracks once again, as John's quiet though insistent drawl joined the fray, reciting from his own poem:

> So we appeal to you, Sun, on this broad day.
> You were ever a helpmate in times of great churning, and
> > fatigue.
> You make us forget how serious we are
> And we dance in the lightning of your rhythm…

"There," continued the resurgent John, "is your time, duration, and your sun all in one."

The whole class broke into laughter, and Professor Bloom, doubtful at first, was soon chuckling also. Judging by what he said after the gaiety abated, however, he had not understood the context of the humor. "Context counts for much," he said, slapping the obvious together from what had moments earlier been slapstick, "and what is Mr. Ashbery to do, since Blake's poem is still alive two centuries later? The only way he can wrestle fairly with Blake's influence is to disguise himself in the voice of Blake's girl,

> The honey of her Infant lips
> The bread & wine of her sweet smile
> The wild game of her roving Eye
> Does him to Infancy beguile

"Harold, Harold," called out David Shapiro beside me, "it's not a trope of voices, it's a play on the idea of a contest itself. I'm looking at the pages of John's poem you gave out yourself,

> If the contest was over, nowhere
> had not been told so. Time's evening relish,
> hole of the great world, came to ice over
> in morning-glory privies where no starlight is,
> no autograph sessions, no costume contest.

"May I say something to mediate?" I asked for I believe the only time (it was understood that as Bloom's collaborator I was present but invisible). "Perhaps, as John makes clear, context is everything and not just a frame. So the poem pulls the frame into the picture as well. Blake's mythmaking creates a context, but John's poem is always enlarging whatever context there is, like collage technique."

I had rung the Bloom buzz-word, "enlargement," thinking to provide him a way out of his predicament: being sandwiched between the great poets of that day, Ginsberg as Blakean herald, Ashbery as arch anti-Academic. The need to enlarge himself to their proportions was as obvious as Bloom's great head and girth. He liked everything in big portions: big cities, big screen TV, big books. Eliot's *The Waste Land* was too small for him, and even though it rivaled Dante in length, Pound's *The Cantos* were "too thin." But Bloom ignored my cue and reshuffled his lecture notes, apparently assigning the joke and the train of thought he had missed to girlhood.

"Menstruation," he countered (and Bloom's gambit was always to introduce a subject as yet on no one's mind), "usually arrives before the serious enlarging of breasts and buttocks." One could sense the breasts in the room perking up. "The result is that the blood—the strength of poetry—has preceded rather than caused the enlargement. In this way, girlhood supercedes the conventional model of strong, classic poetry based upon the engorgement of the phallus with blood. Surely that is what the poem "Girls on the Classics" has in mind. What is conventionally the weak female now becomes, in Mr. Ashbery's enlargement, a band of strong interpreters of the classic male stance manifested in the "mental traveling" of Blake's poem, where the mind stands in for the phallus. The dominant trope thus becomes the word *on*—that is, the "Girls on the Classics" are literally and figuratively bestride them.

> Dream lover, won't you be my darling?
> It's not too late or too early…"

And

> I was only practicing my wail
> thought the witch. This really is unfortunate.
> Same goes for all the centuries we wafted over to get here.

"The blood of the phallus has been outwitted by the blood of the girl, in Mr. Ashbery's enlarged imagination. He has turned the menstrual moon against the sun, and covered his tracks with the classic and ancient canard about female wisdom:

> Now it was Phoebe's turn to complain. "Whoever thinks he can outwit the sun is in for a rude awakening."

"Far from outwitting," he continued, "the girl has in fact enveloped the male—and by his member will be awakened, rather than the other way round. Blake has prepared the ground, and Mr. Ashbery has sat on it, so to speak. At this all-too-obvious pun, Bloom stretched a mock hand of embarrassment across his mouth. The class stared at him as if at a precocious gorilla. There was little left for John or anyone to say. Even Allen was scratching his pate. His anticipatory genius sensing it, Bloom veered unexpectedly to *Kaddish*.

"Since we have the double pleasure of Mr. Ginsberg's company today, let us consider the subject and inspiration of that poem: the mother-figure who has regressed to a form of mad girlhood. Mr. Ginsberg has turned the male duty of reciting the prayer for the dead father, the Kaddish, inside-out in the Blakean manner, with the girlish Naomi—"

"Martin Buberish, to be sure," interjected Ginsberg. "You sound like you've had the same conversation with him I had! He told me he was interested in man-to-man relationships—it was a human universe we were destined to inhabit. Even the nonhuman was "thou," I and thou, and that's all you're doing with my poem. So Naomi's a girl—she's still a human figure for you. But in that poem I was thinking like loss of identity and confrontation with nonhuman universe as the main problem, and in a sense whether or not man had to evolve and change, and perhaps become nonhuman too."

"Wonderfully apropos, Mr. Ginsberg." Bloom was strangely delighted. "Ashbery's girls are refusing the human too by not growing up. They are looking instead for another way to evolve.

> O the moon shines bright on the birdbath
> as on a summer's stream, and we pass slowly from view
> borne by the tide's single-mindedness, and come to seem
>   happy
> as birds frolic, words wuther…

"Moon and menstruation converge again with the tide, so that it's a menstrual tide in tune with birds—the nonhuman, surely."

Now Michal Govrin jumped in, a woman's voice at last. "You could say that the Ashbery poem is also to his girlish mother. Like Ginsberg's Naomi, she also does not menstruate—this is the point, I think, and it is a man's misinterpretation to be always looking for blood. The poem is a kind of exposure of Ashbery's love for his mother, the purity of her origin, the foundation of his being—just as the classics represent a poet's origin."

"Michal is right." It was David Shapiro to her rescue. "Because the source of Ashbery's poem in the literary sense is Rafael Alberti's great book of 1929, *Concerning the Angels*, in which he speaks to a band of girlish angels throughout. Mother was an angel for John, and that is the purity of which Michal speaks. John, no offense; it is a great sublimation you've made. It's because I translated Alberti and know that you have read it (you thanked me for sending the book to you!) that I can testify to it.

> Tras de mi, imperceptible,
> Sin rozarme los hombres,
> Mi angel muerto, vigia.
>
> Behind me, imperceptible,
> Hovering just above my shoulders,
> My dead angel, mothering.

"That is from his poem, 'Paradise Lost,' and also: 'In your orbit my blood was burning, enemy moon'—prefiguring the sublime theme of menstruation that Harold has been uncovering."

"A sublimation it is," added Bloom, reduced to a shockingly nondominant role, a "master of ceremonies" to real authors brought to an articulate boil in an academic hothouse.

John was shrinking further into his seat by the minute. I recalled the earlier "Hi David" he gave me and how I was disarmed. John had never called me David before, only the nickname our colleague, the poet Kenward Elmslie liked to use, "Rosey." It was as if John was appealing for my support in holding the line against exposure—the exposure that visiting the class represented. And then to find himself in tandem with Allen Ginsberg, a poet for whom exposure was as freely given as John's fear of it was guarded… It was not hard to understand how all of John's imaginative powers were now focused upon the wish to disappear.

Yet Bloom turned to John, failing to note the pale cast to his face, and asked, "You don't mind our appreciation for the rational basis of the poem, do you, Mr. Ashbery? Certainly you would agree it is the most rational of Ashberian poems in many years?"

Now John did something unexpected. He uncoiled from his near-fetal position, leapt to his feet, and declaimed the following as if it were a prepared riposte, silently nurtured for years: "Some have viewed it as a temporary 'return to reason' on my part, but I don't think so. I firmly believe in the irrationality of poetry."

"I see," harrumphed Professor Bloom. "Nevertheless—"

"Not fair!" countered Ginsberg. "No emendation needed. First thought best thought."

"Well, I've never subscribed to that," blustered Bloom. "In fact, strong art is revisionist. The art is in the revision."

Latching onto anything to help John out of his predicament, Shapiro rejoined: "*Transparent* revision."

"Yes, naked!" added Allen.

"Revision is ingested by the visionary," continued David, "a conscious appropriation of the dead, or dead classics. It's parental, but unthinking, instinctual."

Come to think of it, Shapiro was the only player in this somewhat Elizabethan literary masque who might be called a proud father. His son Daniel had collaborated with him on poems that were the envy of many.

"Do we need to know about Shakespeare's children?" Bloom responded in mock-inquiry. "Parental, I think not."

"What about Stein, our greatest literary parent of what we could call "classic modern?" David would not let go.

The class hesitated for a moment, considering whether Shapiro might be troping on Gertrude Stein's gayness. Then Allen trumped all stances by interposing a haiku-type quotation of Blake:

"'The child is father to the man,'" he intoned. "And I am father to Naomi! Perhaps this will help next week!"

This time, the class giggled in chorus as never before—as if seeing their own face in the mirror.

It was Michal Govrin, the Israeli, who broke the spell. "I must stand up for the seriousness of Ginsberg here and his deeply Jewish defense of the mother. To trope on honoring the father—and even the medieval Kaddish prayer is blinded here—is to miss Ginsberg's re-parenting of the oldest classic, the Hebrew Bible's 'Honor Thy Father and Mother.'"

Bloom pounded emphatically on the lectern as he finally embodied the stance for which he is justly famous, that of paternal fond correction. "A wonderful commentary, my dear," he said, nodding toward Govrin, seated to my left. "Strangely Buber-like. But I have been thinking of the earlier comment on Martin Buber, his all-too-human stance, and it must now be said that all stances are fragile. Parenting can never be the same again without solid ground to stand on. It is all too late, my dears," he said, turning now to the class at large, pre-empting his guests.

"The very planet we stand on is no longer terra firma, thanks to what once seen can never be forgotten: we are all, human and nonhuman, standing on a fragile planet with no time left to escape. The classics are ever more precious for reminding us how belated we are now, how much ground has been lost, how the room to enlarge ourselves has been usurped by girls—er, excuse me dears, I meant of course the nonhuman. And now we know: even Blake was too late.

> And on the desert wild they both
> Wander in terror & dismay
>
> Like the wild Stag she flees away
> Her fear plants many a thicket wild
> While he persues her night & day
> By various arts of Love beguild
>
> By various arts of Love & Hate
> Till the wide desert planted oer
> With Labyrinths of wayward Love
> Where roams the Lion Wolf & Boar

"There it was, and I admit I did not see it in all my years of 'mental traveling.' The desert of all our losses was the nonhuman Garden of Eden, the one preceding our introduction into it, the one which perhaps did not need our 'planting it oer,' the one in which we had already arrived too late."

He continued on, unimpeded, almost chanting with a Ginsbergian exuberance. "Now we know it is no longer to the fragile present we can look for a foothold, but to the future. I'm sorry, Mr. Ginsberg, but to change our consciousness, or to enact a new language, or to slough off the skin of canonical lyric—none of this can save us anymore. Instead we must pass over the pathos of death itself and imagine a future we will not live to attain, nor even perhaps our species. Rather, we will be looked back upon in fondness—we will become 'as the apple of the eye'— by the next in the ever-growing historical lineage of hominid species, Homo x. It is a post-Homo sapiens poetics of the future, a visionary poetics, that we will need, a nonhuman vision that had been out of fashion long before Blake reminded us two centuries ago. We have had many reminders since, including those by our venerable guests in the room today.

"Let us rejoin our 'plucky band of little girls' to conclude with a final passage from 'Girls on the Classics':

> A horse wanders away
> and is abruptly inducted into the carousel,
> eyes flying, mane askew. There is no end to the dance,
> even death pales in comparison.

"What is revealed to us here is that, as for the horse that we Homo sapiens domesticated, all that is left to us now is flying. We may fly off the planet and into big space, yes, but flying is a trope for leaving.

There is no end to the leaving, the dance of goodbye to the plants and animals of our Eden on earth. And who can we be past the leaving, past postmodern, arriving in the post-enlargement of breasts and buttocks to find the girls we left behind ever more precious, existing only in our poetry, and the classics withering in our hands like useless paper, to be saved and prized only in that future poetry that will no longer stand on the ground, but will be at home in its flying."

At first, some of the students' arms shot up reflexively, as if in scholastic salute, but then they fell back limp, surrendering to the bell that at this graduate level no longer rang but which Professor Bloom had nonetheless rung imaginatively. As we all rose to leave (and now, any form of leavetaking had been heightened) as if leaving the planet, Ashbery and Ginsberg shook their heads at each other in knowledge that neither their fears nor their ecstatic presence remained behind, but only a mutual suspicion of having been frisked by a prurient authority, perhaps.

Bloom had the girls on the run alright, and the fleeting grandiosity of having been encompassed with the classics was ripped away from the band of poets like a flimsy skirt. This had been a day in which we felt the blood rising in our heads, only to realize that we were no different than the pre-menstrual girls of

Ashbery's poem, inexperienced with the lustful intentions of the classics lurking beneath them.

THE PROPHETIC POET
OF THE TWENTIETH CENTURY[1]

In the spring of 2001 I flew up to Vancouver to work in the bpNichol Archive at Simon Fraser University and to give a lecture on the great North American poet of my generation. Due to the unexpectedly sharp and insistent questions that followed the lecture, I agreed to extend the presentation into another day. Many of those present had known bpNichol while he was alive and some were old friends of mine. In the end, my initial lecture turned into a weeklong series. Each day I pushed toward closure, only to find that glaring questions remained. These questions are incorporated and addressed in each succeeding day's lecture.

It came to me that what we have lost are the seven days of creation. These contain the instinctive knowledge that we were the last primate species to evolve and that what we have most left behind in the Garden is not a fantasy of childhood but rather our parental species. We are orphans, as it were, searching through time for our lost parents, who all the while *remain part of the framing natural landscape in which we live, dressed up as trees or mountains or worms.*

> "deny ourselves we deny our gods…
> only the man trapped in words recognizes that futility"
> The Martyrology

DAY ONE. SUNDAY.

The initial lecture was postponed by an unprecedented transit strike. By 10 A.M. on Sunday the downtown streets were clogged with more vehicles than had ever descended there. I was stranded at the oceanfront Hotel Sylvia, historical artifact and cousin to New York's Hotel Chelsea, dawdling over a late breakfast with the benefit only of the Friday edition of the Vancouver Sun and its anachronistic headline, "Strike Averted In Last Minutes," when I was surprised by a silver-haired Tony Curtis lookalike standing beside me and peering over my shoulder. "Rosenberg, I presume?" he said. He had that Tony Curtis quizzical look. It was Jamie Reid, who explained he had made it in from North Vancouver by parking his car on the other side of the bridge and hitching rides downtown. "Don't tell my wife," he whispered.

A former radical union organizer who auditioned first by co-organizing the legendary Vancouver International Poetry Conference in the early sixties and co-founding

TISH magazine, Jamie sat down and within minutes was describing his organizing work for the 40th Anniversary of that conference, at which Robin Blaser would be standing in for Robert Duncan and George Stanley for Jack Spicer—that many were "still standing" was the underlying memo. Jamie further explained that he felt duty-bound to guide my walking trip into Stanley Park, where I had earlier on the phone described my desire to find the relatively untouched forest I had visited thirty years ago, with sustaining memories of radically diverse species of birds and small mammals. "Nothing but rats and pigeons now," he cautioned.

"The orcas in the new Aquarium?" I offered.

"They charge admission," Jamie said, scowling.

"Then it'll have to be the Totem Poles," I insisted. "And they're free." This had in fact been my first wish but they had been described as too far to reach on foot, at least for athletes in retirement such as ourselves. Somehow we made it, twice stopping out of breath to pretend to savor the ocean view largely obscured by fog.

They were overwhelming, and infinitely more poignant than the last time I saw them. While Jamie felt duty-bound to explain the symbolism of all the animals long fled and represented upon them, it was the wildness of the Indians themselves that shook me, their presence luminous behind the poles and outrageous, as if backlit fluorescent light had been invented by them in the nineteenth century. To these Indian artists, it was I who was the paleface destroyer of the forest, and in a last, desperate attempt at translating wildness into art, I would be made to turn and flee—or at least learn reverence—before this wild power. Now, barely a century since their last stand, parents were explaining the huge, winged poles to their children as a domestic fantasy—as if this remnant of a primitive Disneyland was created out of human camaraderie. I looked into the mother eagle's face and wanted to flee with her, on her back, out of shame. The pole was still wild.

Day Two. Monday.

bpNichol is the great translator-in-disguise of the 20th century. His oeuvre of over forty books consists largely of disguised translations from the Sumerian of the great court poet of King Shulgi at Ur in the late third millennium and down to others at the court of King Hammurapi in the 18th century BCE. The original poet in Ur, a translator himself, is known only to a tiny coterie of scholars by the capitalized initials, BP.

For reasons that are only now becoming clear, Nichol never let on that his works were translations, although many hints are scattered throughout the oeuvre, especially in the nine books of *The*

Matryrology. While the latter has been acclaimed by Canadian critics as the major epic of the second half of the 20th century, it is in fact largely a restoration of a series of Sumerian epic fragments ascribed to BP and built upon a quest for immortality in writing, which formed the basis for the original *Epic of Gilgamesh*.

It is not hard to understand why Nichol remained in disguise. The opprobrium upon his head in Canada had he told all (and the consequent status of outcast) would have sunk his career. In Canada, the art of translation from poets of the past is considered the joint obligation of the U.S. and the United Kingdom. Translations by poets of Virgil or *Beowulf* are not emanating from India, South Africa, or any other former Commonwealth outpost. It was hard enough for a Canadian writer just to assert her existence in the 20th century. "Let the Americans do it!" comes the imagined reply to a Canadian poet's grant request to translate Dante. "The Americans have no further need to prove their existence in our century."

However, not even an American poet would consider learning cuneiform in order to translate Sumerian, and only in the 1990s did an indifferent academic poet, David Ferry, translate a pastiche version of the *Epic of Gilgamesh*. To be sure, Professor Ferry acknowledged that he had not spent a moment of his busy American time studying cuneiform but rather had examined two or three mediocre translations by scholars. Even Ezra Pound had made an effort to understand the Chinese ideogram.

Why can't just one U.S. poet admit to learning cuneiform?[2] For one very good reason. Sigmund Freud notwithstanding, the origin of written poetry remains a taboo, enforced by conventions dating back to Christian Humanist ideas of classical, divine, and other forms of inspiration. Prehistorical oral poetry has had a recent vogue, but the original "scene of writing"—the Sumerian occasions when an oral poet studied to be a scribe, on one hand, and a scholarly scribe found himself writing poetry on the other—is as verboten to the modern imagination as mommy and daddy's conjugal bed. Lest we forget, the biblical *Book of Job* had no trouble pointing out the primal sexual scene.

Few poets are conscious of the prohibition against imagining the ur-text of written poetry. Admit it—and face a poem which would have no written "tradition" to either uphold or subvert, an impossible position for contemporary writers. For them, an urtext can only be imagined as a reflected posterior of their own work.

But bpNichol found sanction to learn cuneiform in the guise of an experimental *artist*, circumventing the taboos associated with written poetry. In the late 1960s, some of us tried to challenge the idea of a received "poem"; we referred to our poetic output as "works" in order to blur boundaries between literary, artistic, musical and theoretical composition. The subsequent French preference for "texts" as a term of genre-blurring has become normative; still, in the realm of theory, tradition is quick to reassert itself. Adopting the disguise of an experimental poet allowed bpNichol to be easily situated in the older avant garde tradition that encompassed Pound's ancient Chinese translations and Charles Olson's Mayan studies of the 1950s. Behind this literary duckblind, Nichol could seek the origins of written poetry in the history of the alphabet and its glyphic roots in pre-Mediterranean languages—all the way back to Sumer, to which references peek out from the elaborate costume of *The Martyrology*. What appears to be a postmodern experiment conjoining ancient epic and modern serial poem is in fact an intricate disguise, more sophisticated than the personal masquerade the rest of us carry on for the sake of our inner lives. *The Martyrology* allowed Nichol to become not only the most original translator in the history of the English language but also to overshadow the increasingly recherche tendencies in American and British letters.

The rediscovery that the art of writing is founded upon the act of translation is bpNichol's gift to the twentieth century—that, and how the complex of sound, smell, taste, touch and sight comes together again at certain sublime points after the post-humanist disorderings of the senses. In the same way, the original poet spoke from a new unity, the words forming a body of their own: a translation of the primal body. To recognize this new body is to be foretold the future of our species. In whatever way this translated body's story progresses—and the story is largely irrelevant—we become aware that we are listening as if to a new species. So that the real story is of our listening and offering up our own bodies to be translated.

bpNichol insinuated himself into the modern experimental tradition by appropriating the most marginal of its figures, Jarry, Ball, and Dick Higgins among them. But it was Duchamp that he most resembled, the trajectory of whose work remained invisible until it became posthumous. Each required that their work seem already posthumous while they are still alive, a protective disguise. It was actually their bodies that were the work and not the reverse— or the reconstruction of a body projected into the future and looking back at us, and at itself, its former body. During their lifetimes, no one is aware of it. Later, we come to understand that the body of work by Duchamp or Nichol contains, as it were, a new species we are listening to. In the case of bpNichol, we are still approaching the future he embodied, one in which the organization of the senses is reconstituted from a social identity into a new familiarity with isolation.

Like Proust, Nichol pulls a forgotten universe, a "cloud town," out of memory. While Proust's world showed us first where we are, Nichol is concerned from the outset with who we might become. We have few writers who share this concern and are capable of embodying it. Just finding the necessary point of isolation is beyond comprehension, and I couldn't begin to conceive of it until I was almost fifty. Yet bp was barely in his twenties when the path opened for him. It can't be a conscious isolation or any form of social isolation (including common twentieth century metaphors of alienation and anxiety). The greatest visionary we have ever had was the original, estranged one, right there at the origin of writing, who in the process of translating oral into written poetry blazed a trail of who we might become. By giving us back this true original, Nichol shocks us awake to the possibility of seeing further into our prehistory—all the way back to the scene of becoming human.

That primal scene is no longer covered by the blinding cliché of a time when we became "civilized," diverting us from looking further. Instead, the earlier "scene of evolving" was the point of utter isolation during which Homo sapiens looked into the eyes and listened to the circumscribed speech of whom he or she had been (Neandertal, Homo Habilus) and saw he must explore the world anew.

We are pointed toward this prehistory and future as bpNichol brings us to the original scene of writing. But how? Nothing he could say or describe could change us, just as science or science fiction cannot, until we experience the new world for ourselves. First, in other words, we must change, and Nichol shows the way by disguising his revelation in the severe playfulness of an experimental writer. This performance is so extreme that it shields the author and protects him from being appropriated by the literary world, or from being misunderstood as someone who is showing us who we are (the first ambition of all conservative writers). There is no mistaking bp, no possibility of swallowing him into the mainstream or Western canon; he will always stick in the throat, inassimilable, to be thrown out again into the wildness of a new present. Perhaps fifty years from now will make that clear, perhaps a hundred and fifty.

When bpNichol can be read with the disguise put aside and the hidden BP clear, his life after death will become apparent. His afterlife consists in the abolishment of time between himself and the original BP, and between ourselves and the primal scene of evolving Homo sapiens. As the original translator BP in Sumer is revealed, he or she is himself translated, so that the irony of a personal death inheres in a selfhood that had already been made free. BP was free from it while alive in Sumer: the scene of writing is revealed in the translation made from hearing a voice to writing a voice—an inscribed voice that can be "heard" until the end of time.

As visionary writers, both the Sumerian BP and bpNichol are explorers of the future. We readers also carry visionary sparks in our wish to be reborn—or what we usually call a hope for a new life, or to live through our children's lives, or simply the hope that good luck will change our lives. This wish resides in memory, where we remember our former lives outlived. We wish to again and again be reborn in order to explore the world anew, but unfortunately this happens to most of us in a form of cultural consumerism: tourism, for one, or building up our careers or estate. The explorations of the visionary writer involve new ways of thinking—ways under immediate threat of assimilation, of being fit into or onto an existing mode of thought that will domesticate its wildness. In order to preserve its potency, which resides in its wildness, this writer needs a disguise. The old forms of sanction for such wildness, the roles of prophet and shaman and visionary, are gone, reduced to the irony of metaphors for trendsetting. What is left is the embodiment of the translator.

Later in the afternoon of the first day, Sunday, back at the Sylvia, Jamie said goodbye as he pointed me in the direction of Bill Bissett's new apartment, just a short block away. Bill embraced me in a long bear hug, although I recalled we had met only rarely, back in Toronto at the Coach House, introduced by bp. "I was at Rochdale that whole summer," he explained, referring to the experimental college in which I was allotted a "resource persons" apartment. "I had such a tremendous crush on you I was afraid to approach you." Now he himself was an established experimental institution in Canada, a living totem of bp, his younger friend and colleague from the beginning.

But Bill was not the same. He had fallen down an empty elevator shaft during an artists loft party; he had been in a coma and was written off. A young woman doctor, however, tried experimental brain surgery and after nine months of "rehab" he was a new man. "It's like I'm Bill Bissett in disguise and inside I'm more relaxed and focused. He's a voice in my head, so the new writing is like I'm translating Bill Bissett. Being a translator I feel like a regular person for the first time, someone with a real job."

DAY THREE. TUESDAY.

Let us review where it was we began. I've discussed bpNichol's disguise as an experimental poet and mentioned my own as a translator. The wildness beneath the disguise I have called the lost "scene of writing," where an ungovernable, or wild, form of translation had begun. For BP in Sumer, it was oral into written; for bp and myself it continues in re-creating this scene within the problematics of authorship, of embodying a lost author. The wildness of that first scene allows through it an echo of having evolved. What we know—and what we find—is that our original translation took place from a less language-obsessed earlier species into Homo sapiens.

Human culture estranges us from this nonhuman prehistory, but part of our genome has always continued to mutate toward the nonhuman again. We are in touch with it when sensing that the future of human identity is to return to a Garden of Eden, a nonhuman ecosystem in which the loss of our humanity—which is always seen as a catastrophe by false prophets—will become a form of progress. This non-catastrophe is an event in which we evolve naturally and trust the nonhuman again; it will seem more natural than the idea of an Earth in our image, a global hive of cities and states, town and pacified country, and the putting on of a prosthesis to get around virtually anywhere.

Within our human monocultures, the nonhuman element we trust the most is time; that is, as I (allow me to speak for us a moment) accept myths of the future I'm able to diminish the power of time to merely a frame holding us, a picture frame that we exclude from the picture itself. I try to assimilate—to neutralize or domesticate—any nonhuman element that enters the frame. If I can't, this wild stuff is suppressed by labeling it incoherent or childish (although personally, I might call it subversive), just as the modern art of abstraction in painting was first called. Today, this art too has been domesticated and become part of the window-dressing of human culture, permeating everything from clothes to web sites.

I wouldn't like to think of myself as so rigid, but no one can easily avoid the "us" of human cultures. The same domestication happens to our memories, both personal and collective. Essentially, anything in the past is also nonhuman to us, beyond human power to retrieve, except as it is civilized in dramatic plots of history and myth. Without these cultural or religious stories, accompanied by some form of imagined afterlife ("the spirits of the past"), we are estranged from history. It takes only a wild thought to remind us of it; otherwise, we imagine we are on some form of direct or cyclical progression from the past.

Take the Yahwist, the J writer of the early Bible. Like the prophet Abraham of whom she writes, she also represents a new way of thinking. The wildness of it in fact has been preserved in the removal of her identity and the erasure of the scene of writing, which had for her been a creative translating of older cuneiform tablets as well as oral verse into the new Hebraic alphabet. We may assume as well that after the time of J's writing in Solomonic Jerusalem, her first interpreters tried to domesticate her work. Only after many generations of weak commentary was it proved inassimilable, so that "it seems to be true." Once accepted as such, her writing could then be assimilated as a kind of history to be believed.

The same must have happened to the Sumerian BP and can happen again to the great bp of our time. After the current mainstream falls away (to which he seems provincial, a "Canadian," although with international pretensions) a new mainstream in which he remains inassimilable will reveal that he stands apart. Perhaps he will form the backbone of a new "sacred" canon, one in which Canada seems central for being just as marginal as biblical Israel once was, sandwiched between the dominant Egyptian and Sumerian-Akkadian-Babylonian cultures of its day.

Meanwhile, those authors today whose work remains free are challenged either as outlaws or (as the culture's assimilated outlaws are called) "geniuses": Blake, Rimbaud, Stein among them. The wild aspect of their originality retains a mysterious connection to the primal and taboo scene of writing. To the mainstream, their vision appears as if sprung from nowhere, as if they were translating an unknown original. More concerned with the fate of species than the self-regarding grandiose question of "What is a human life?" (as if it stood apart from other species) the visionary poet faces an evolutionary future.

bpNichol and I came of age in an apocalyptic moment of the sixties, when it seemed that whatever the future would be, it would be different. It did not occur to me that the consequent disregard for the contemporary culture (we stole books, lied on grant proposals, etc.—what did it matter?) was typical of any outlaw, the majority of whom were not interested in any future at all. bp understood faster than anybody that the future had to be explored in the deep past. Eventually I became a translator too, although my costume was less perfect than bp's. Ignored by the avant garde, it became quickly clear to me that any legitimate avant garde history would not include writers in sublime disguises. There would be no room for the late, wild Thoreau, for instance. For the avant garde's interest was not really in changing—in learning to read the acorn and the huckleberry—but in protecting the human capital of an experimental canon.

"The cultural dichotomies between writing & speech—the 'written' & the 'oral'—disappear the closer we get to the source," writes Jerome Rothenberg, introducing *A Book of the Book* (2001). "There is a primal book as there is a primal voice, & it is the task of our poetry & art to recover it....That recovery, of course, is also a matter of demonstration....of where such a view *might lead* us....but without the real hope or even the desire to bring it to conclusion." Where that might lead is out, out to the natural world, but that is not where *this* avant garde is going. That would be too conclusive. In other words, the scene of evolving in the natural world would then overshadow the scene of writing at the "source," diminishing the grandiosity of poets as well. So what is missing here is an understanding of the crucial act of translation at the original scene of the "writing" of our species. Later, at the literal human moment of incision upon wet clay, the writing and speech did not melt into each other but rather an act of insemination was required, a primal scene in which the intercourse—the translation—is not screened out.

What is this act? Our species has a voice like many other species. Birds can sing and rattlesnakes rattle. If there is a possible avant garde, it is in the hope that we can overcome the pomposity of our sounds: the invention of writing led the way when the first poetry was written in Sumer. All the visionary poetry written since then has served to remind us of our increasing isolation. The genuine poetry has been subversive; far from serving culture, it has helped break it down by unmasking our isolation from the natural world and from our species consciousness.

Rothenberg, himself a significant translator, concludes that "the return to the book is the step now needed to make the work complete," assuming that perhaps the avant garde has too much explored the voice. But what a sad defeat that would be. That is why the time has come to expose and acknowledge the genius of bpNichol, whose work might at first seem to point from the page to the voice, and from the visual to the page, but which in fact points from the page to the wood—to the true origins of natural species. Beyond the forest origin of the fibrous page, Rothenberg might have more judiciously written "the return to clay is the step now needed," for it is the clay tablets on which Gilgamesh and other Sumerian poetry was first committed to an unknown future that it became possible to survive our species and be read in an indeterminate future. bp's return to the clay tablet is a gesture toward the scene of evolving and the buried knowledge of it in the act of translation.

Between the oral and the book is the translating mind's singular voice-in-the-head, a consciously species-wide voice. In Book Two of *The Martyrology*, Nichol points to the conflated time and space of our origin, "the one voice vision":

> "there is a music in the moment comes together
> joyce thot he knew or that insistence stein found
> approximation of the one voice vision..."

This vision understands creation as the one addressee, the one word in which all are contained—and from which all are translated. It's the word spoken by our fathering species, the one preceding us, which we proceeded to translate with our voice-in-the-head just as the Homo x species that will outlive our extinction will translate ours with its similar voice-in-the-head:

> "nothing matters but that He has created
> & we sing Him his praises"

Nichol here brings back the Sumerian creator who has made many drafts of his earthly creation before us and many new species in the same manner to come after us.

On the night of the first day, Sunday, Victor Coleman flew in and talked a policewoman into a ride to the hotel. Victor had set bp's books, my books, and also his own intricately impassioned volumes on the Coach House linotype. We exchanged token presents in the Sylvia's cork-lined "postcard-writing room." His was a copy of the just-published restoration in one volume of *The Great Canadian Sonnet*, an impossibly buoyant and classic novel by David McFadden with collaborative drawings on facing pages by Greg Curnoe, typeset by Victor and printed in miniature format. It went through several printings when published in '71, split into two volumes because the glue in those days was too brittle to properly bind such a thick miniature book. Even so, the pages started falling out before one could finish.

Victor bounced the book forcefully on the floor, a startling act since he was so very sensitive to books and this one in particular now belonged to me. I expected to see it fly apart like in the old days. "See?" said Victor.

"See what?" I responded, not sure the lesson was that simple.

"It took thirty years for the technology to catch up," he said.

It was a beautiful little book, a "real" book now, but soon we were talking about the old days and how everything flew apart then, and in particular the acid trip we shared in a Dufferin County forest. For the first time, it was good to feel as if I was someone else, not even human, an intelligent animal wandered into a vast living library. I could read the text of the air itself, inscribed by light with the letters of small flying things—in the twilight the tiny flies were dancing—and then the surprise of the human, Victor and others I've forgotten, standing around and watching everything too, as if we'd all just evolved and still understood that other species were reading us too. What a relief to find each tree with its own intelligence, processing light, its unrepressed history written in its height and reach. Unmasked, I felt part of a community of species.

And then it was dark. As we scrambled for the car, it became apparent to me we had not brought a designated driver. It was my Rambler, but as I took the wheel it seemed to break off in my hands. I didn't tell anybody this; instead, I translated: We're going to have to wait here a couple hours while the battery re-charges. Nobody challenged me. It was a perfect translation.

Day Four. Wednesday.

Take a step back a moment, toward a Nichol forerunner. Emily Dickinson's work may appear the height of civilization but her ultimate assimilability is wild and always in question. No oral poetry could accomplish that. Close to other species, aware of their companion voices, Dickinson's isolation was not so much disguised as literal.

What was missing in oral poetry? It was the necessary displacement in translation, the act of moving from the human voice to the nonhuman representation of it. The final result, the written poetry itself, is only visionary to the extent that it reveals the necessity of that translation—and the consequent isolation that a written tablet, page or screen brings. It is in the act of translation that we are closest to the wildness of natural selection and the scene of our evolving. Most translations from one language into another are only a pale reflection of this, but a few, those opening onto the original scene of translation from oral into written, are seminal and usually appear in a necessary disguise.

Consider the visionary prose poetry of Thoreau's late journals, which first appear to be in the form of diaristic writings, autobiographical notes, or scientific investigations. When re-published today, they are described as forerunners of the recent science of ecology—proving that as poetry they remain inassimilable and worthy of their disguise. For Thoreau's *Journals*, too, are translations, and have had to remain hidden or succumb to the taboo still in force against coming face to face with other species. Such an encounter might rob us of our species grandiosity (heaven forbid). True, the work of Rothenberg, among others, helps to deflate our *cultural* grandiosity, but that is a poor substitute for exposing our repression of primal ground, as can come clear in a sublime translation *of* the original scene of writing. Rimbaud was such a translator but he was too young and inexperienced to develop a disguise, and it was soon too late for him to explore the source material for translation that bp found and continually researched, fueling a lifelong work.

In his fine introduction to *Selected Poems of Solomon Ibn Gabirol* (2001), the poet Peter Cole excavates a medieval "age of translation" that echoes the Solomonic composition of the early Bible. "Translation, particularly in an age of translation, is not only what hired or inspired workers have rendered into another language; it is also what writers who read in multiple languages translate in thought alone—the force of which is brought to bear on the written language they use. This, granted, is simply influence; in this instance, however, it is influence born of a steady passage across linguistic and regional borders."

Canada was such a place in our time, where "an age of translation" was more transparently an age of crossing the borders of genre. The Canadian poets I knew read and wrote in multiple genres. Ondaatje,

Atwood, and the resurgent Anne Carson are popular examples, but there are many more who are less well known internationally, Bowering, McCaffery, the promising Werschler-Henry—though none more significantly unknown in the whole of the twentieth century than bpNichol. It is a testimony to Nichol's disguise that in Canada itself he is known primarily as a miner of dozens of genres, for that is a big deal in "mainstream" Canada though hardly the real deal. Underneath *The Martyrology* lies the singular genre of visionary poetry and its origin at the scene of writing, in Ur.

Unlike ordinary writers, the poet as original translator doesn't so much imagine the future as explore it by re-imagining a buried past, one that every culture is based upon defeating and becoming superior to. All except the primal culture, that is, the one with no preceding tradition besides evolution itself. To see ourselves differently, the taboos against probing prehistory have to be imaginatively undermined. It is not easy to show the ways in which we are derived from—and therefore lesser than—"the primitive." It can't be done in the open, where most writers find themselves, but rather in the guise of a prophet whom we follow because we mistake him or her as a translator, an invisible presence, and thus read instead an anonymous text from the past, unbeknownst, one that originates at the scene of writing but which we are innocent of knowing. Just as we prefer to be innocent of our parents' primal bed, we prefer to imagine the prophet as a type of saint or asexual scribe, his or her text born immaculately.

Once the original writing was set in stone, it became universal in a new way. And once it was read, we were changed, knowing in our conscious minds that it could now be translated into any other language at any time, such as a future time where our own language is extinct. Previously, the oral text depended on the presence of the poet himself, or one standing in for him. Now, a poet can imagine our own species extinction while the poem itself may survive. Even to the Sumerian, the knowledge embedded in the clay tablet implied another culture reading it upon the extinction of Sumer, a superceding culture that would have seemed as strange to it as another species.

On almost every page of *The Martyrology*, bpNichol finds himself in a world where everything is new, Edenic, as if he were a new species. Even the paper before him is newly strange, as are the immediate tools of technology and nature surrounding the contemporary scene of writing: pen, typewriter, car, lamp, window, recorded voice. Just as each new technological discovery opened up new routes to the past as well as the possibilities of civilization (just in Sumer: wheel, irrigation, writing) our latest advance is the new listening allowed by bpNichol's translation of the original scene of writing. It authorizes us to imagine what comes next, informed by natural selection.

Not knowing upon going to bed Sunday night whether the strike would be continued into Monday (it wasn't) I arranged to have breakfast in the Sylvia's "Charles Dickens Room" with the poet Gerry Gilbert. Gerry is famous for living on a bicycle with the accoutrements necessary to his urban nomad lifestyle: journal, taperecorder, sketch pad, trail mix, rain gear, and copies of the longest running avant garde poetry magazine in Canada, in which I was published thirty-odd years ago, his "B.C. Monthly." On greeting him, I joked about the strike's end, brought up short by Gerry's puzzlement: what strike? Gerry lived in a more elemental universe perfectly attuned to the next avant garde, an invisible wall-to-wall culture, transparent to ambient sound and light. He hosted the longest running poetry program on radio, "Radio Free Rainforest," which would be broadcasting my lectures "live" (i.e. unedited tape with ambient sound, including the occasional bus returned to circulation and heard accelerating through an open window).

Gerry was also famous for illustrating his own books, each one including his trademark ur-drawing of a healthy Canadian slug in close-up, on the move, with the trace of its trail visible behind it. I recalled the genesis of those drawings in one of Gerry's books from the sixties, brought with him on a visit to Toronto: like a Chinese landscape screen, each page folded out from the previous one, and on each page the slug's progress was noted with minimal verse and drawing of fragments of detritus, hints of the human and the natural, then to fold away behind with each passing page. Paul Valery had written a great essay on snails in the thirties, but Gilbert's little book had surpassed it by revealing the slug's imagined sex life. To this day, ecologists cannot accurately describe how its sexuality unfolds in the wild slug's ecosystem, although I have seen a photograph of slugs observed in a college laboratory, the table on which the terrarium sat surrounded by "Mr. Coffee" machines.

How did slugs evolve and what was their last common ancestor shared with snails? I asked Gerry if he'd thought about this, and as soon as he began to answer I realized the enormity of the scene of evolving: the elaborate shells of snails resembled the most awe-inspiring poetry, according to Valery, and yet the slug found it irrelevant to its more ancient poetry of multiplying the numbers of microscopic "feet" on its single foot.

"It's the metaphor of a home that humans can't get past," Gerry said, with a touch of distaste. "That's why they go for the obvious art of seashells and are dismissive of the slug. But while the snails are busy with technological feats, building fantastic abodes, the slug continues to explore its ground, its research invisible to the grandiosity of humanity but totally necessary to our survival. Waste is turned into fresh organic matter in the slug's digestion, and I have found species of slugs that will break down a book into living matter within the course of their lifetime."

I was loathe to leave the table for my initial lecture that afternoon, but I smiled to myself knowing that bp would have perfectly understood. Besides, Gerry was anxious to move on. We had fully tested his recording gear over a dessert that he had smuggled in himself, a pate preserve of roasted acorns.

DAY FIVE. THURSDAY.

The hidden story of bp's life as a translator is quite simple really, apart from the more complex biography of the experimental writer and artist. I often ran into him in the University of Toronto library and though we exchanged smiles it didn't occur to me to ask what he was researching. "Researching" is what we did, period. So it is likely that bp began studying cuneiform in the special collections of the UT library as early as 1964, when he was employed full time there as a librarian's assistant, and then proceeding with a Jungian therapist well-versed in myth and early texts, at the experimental Therafields community. The therapist (the "Lea" to whom *The Martyrology* is dedicated) died before revealing the scholarly association. The texts bp used would have been the latest twentieth century photocopies of Sumerian tablets, and some originals for comparison, held at the Royal Ontario Museum a few blocks away.

Particularly moving, in retrospect, is Book 5's representation of "the Annex," the neighborhood surrounding the university where bp and I lived and where bp depicts himself walking the streets in the same manner as his Sumerian forebear, BP, walked the streets surrounding Shulgi's court. The Babylonian translation of BP made at Hammurapi's court named the already destroyed streets of sacred Ur—even as this Akkadian translator walked the streets of later Babylon. And bp in modern Toronto played in the same way with the unconscious sacredness attached to streets of the Annex, including the history of their naming and a personal history leading to poignant scenes of driving north into wilder Ontario and as far as the veritable ghost town of Plunkett, Saskatchewan, where his family originally settled and had disappeared from.

One of the Sumerian epics bp translated in fragments, *Gilgamesh*, featured the original "wild man," Enkidu. At one point, in a short book peripheral to *The Martyrology*, Enkidu is translated into Billy the Kid.

> this is the true eventual story of billy the kid.it is not the story as he told it for he did not tell it to me.he told it to others who wrote it down, but not correctly.there is no true eventual story but this one.had he told it to me i would have written a different one.i could not write the true one had he told it to me.

It is quite ironic that for most readers bpNichol seemed so much a product of the sixties that he received Canada's major recognition, the Governor-General's Award, for this very book, entitled "The True Eventual Story of Billy the Kid," while he was still in his twenties. The further irony of replacing a Sumerian mythic hero, Enkidu, with a North American one, italicizes the change in meaning that "wild" has acquired. Instead of "running with wolves" or "drinking with gazelles" as Enkidu had (or even the wildness of an underage drinker of blood, and, not least, the seven days of nonstop sex with a goddess), instead of these depictions of Enkidu, "wildness" now meant running with outlaws or beating mere men to the draw.

We are witness to bp's layering here, the wildness of Enkidu re-emerging in the boast that eventually all other stories of Billy the Kid will appear untrue beside this one, since that is how myth is made. While most of prehistory is a story of the need as well as fear of being civilized,

> ...the true eventual story is that billy and the sheriff were friends.if they had been more aware they would have been lovers.

Like Enkidu and Gilgamesh, wild and civilized, the friendship of Billy and Pat Garrett reaches its climax in death and loss—and the impoverishment of a civilization without memory of that lost wildness.

There's Homer and the two great writers of the early Bible, but first there was Gilgamesh and Enkidu. bp wrote himself into the *Epic of Gilgamesh*, in a transparently autobiographical and lifelong search for the wild comrade or twin, a search that only succeeds if death can be overcome. The secret to immortal life, hidden in the journey itself, necessitates a continual opening out of the poem until it is identical with the poet's body. The death of the poet, then, is not the death or end of the poem but rather the point at which the scene of writing meets the scene of translation. How can this happen in our own time? It happened when bpNichol in *The Martyrology* imagined his death before the event and then translated the poem thus "ended" into a further book—Book Five and onward—where the translator who takes over for "bp" dramatizes the oral becoming written, in the form of how human consciousness becomes species consciousness. bp cannot "die" so much as become translated into the reader of a future species in the Homo line, one whose living body incarnates the scene of translation. Our future reader becomes one with the scene of evolving as he or she reads.

In the first four books of *The Martyrology*, Nichol translated the older Sumerian myth into written testaments of the saints who left heaven for earth; that is, they left their immortal bodies for which the oral was all that was necessary, and came down into the texts themselves, "the stories of their lives", which bp re-animated in translation. Such was their martyrdom. In the later four books it is bp himself who embodies the story and whose selfhood had entered the text earlier in order to be translated.

Waiting to begin the lecture, I scanned the assembling audience. I recognized many but I looked in vain for other poets with whom I'd hoped to reunite in Vancouver: David Phillips, Joe Rosenblatt, Daphne Marlatt and the incomparable Nichol scholar, Irene Niechoda. Renee Rodin was there, and Roy Miki, a major writer on bp, who was sitting at the far edge of his seat, as if trying to avoid the shadow of charm emanating from the Cary Grantish colleague beside him, George Bowering. David Cull and Billy Little also sat side by side, avant garde poets to the last, writing notes on napkins.

I also spotted Goh Poh Seng, renowned Singapore poet in Canadian exile, a magic realist washed up on the Pacific shore. Later, at a party at Poh Seng's house, I asked him what he'd thought of my first lecture. "I understood very little," he said. Then he grabbed my arms and gave me a friendly shaking. "David, I kid you. I understood that you have a very great love for translation, and that the languages do not matter. I did not know him but I felt like I myself was becoming bpNichol. I was feeling at home in Canada, secure with intangible things. I was wondering if words ever had a visible origin and if there were invisible poets who made them to attract isolated ancestors to explore the ends of the earth, just like they made plum trees to attract squirrels far away. These invisible poets will care for our work once we are extinct, yes?"

DAY SIX. FRIDAY.

The New York Times obit for Gertrude Stein, July 27, 1946, quotes "the Hearst press" as asking "Is Gertrude Stein not Gertrude Stein but somebody else living and talking in the same body?" Here is the sense of another writer hidden behind a disguise— and as if this other is a mutation or new species, a portent of new consciousness. As Stein pushed abstraction to its farthest limits, according to the Times, Nichol pushed intelligibility to its limits.

While experimental writing can be abstract, translation is always about intelligibility. And yet, "Miss Stein is a very powerful character and things are apt to change dizzily when translated into Steinese." Here the joke is on the obit writer, in that if "Steinese" is a code, it is at bottom always intelligible, and the key to that code must lie in Gertrude Stein's character and life. In a similar manner, bp's life is constantly entering the work beyond self-contemplation, in the form of friends, relatives, and loves, and since they themselves are translations of ancient relations in Sumer they are not changed into "Nicholese" but remain exactly as they are. We perceive the poet's life at the scene of translation from its oral context into a written text.

Thanks to our knowledge of evolution, we do not consider ourselves for an instant superior to those at the Sumerian or biblical courts. They had their own way to dramatize the scene of evolving as a scene of divine authorship and its translation. The ancient resistance to it, in the form of "oral literary achievement" and a secular canon, is either lost or become translated into "sacred text." What, then, is an author of the sacred? His or her sensibility is one that understands an unknown original has existed, and at the scene of translation this author becomes a visionary poet. Hard as it is to imagine most poets today freed of their addiction to "literary achievement" and able to work with the unknown, it is bpNichol who leads the way in the second half of the twentieth century by having translated the original scene of writing in Sumer into a vision of what is involved in leaving Homo sapiens behind.

Partly this is done by equating the scene of evolving, where our species left behind its predecessors, with the original scene of writing, producing a revelation in *The Martyrology* of how we today hold the self and its linguistic creations sacred in our unconscious life. More immediately, the drama of the mortality of the self—its martyrdom to the wish for immortality in works of art—is placed in the context of the Western canon, which is wholly dependent on the "immortal authorship" of the Bible and its scene of translation into the Latin Vulgate and, preeminently, into the English Bible. All of this is evident in the grand development of the eight books of *The Martyrology* (although not including the posthumous 9th book). But what has been until now hidden is the scene of translation, the visionary return to the original scene of writing in Sumer. For the select readership of *The Martyrology*, limited to an encounter with its small press edition conserved by Toronto's Coach House Books, it has not been necessary to face this revelation for the simple reason of being largely Canadians, that is, "lay" readers unaware of any "church" or orthodoxy and thus free to imagine "giving up selfhood" with the author in a new type of sacred bond. This freedom is denied to Americans, for instance, who are saddled with the sad consciousness of the orthodox Western canon and its liturgy of literary achievement.

I had to become an immigrant twice in order to learn how to resist this secular orthodoxy, including its voracious assimilation of experimental poetry. In Canada, I learned from bp the necessity of an underlying work of translation that is unexposed to the mainstream: an unassimilated page, a sign of words with a different resonance. And in Israel, I stumbled on the meaning of prophecy by becoming assimilated into a contemporary Hebrew culture without being able to expose my personal sense of mission. Both immigrations were a kind of rebirth and so recapitulated the scene of translation—though not, of course, the scene of evolving, where all memory of the past was expunged. Rebirth with memory of the past life was the astonishing visionary future that opened to BP of Ur—and to me as I came into contact with bpNichol, and later, the great biblical writers. Only I did not know it until I re-read *The Martyrology* in the 1990s, after belatedly learning of bp's sudden death in Toronto, and as I began myself to translate from Sumerian cuneiform.

As I've noted, the marginal nature of a Canadian poet allowed bp the freedom to cross artistic boundaries and work in many genres with much less inhibition than his contemporaries in the dominant cultures of America or Europe. I myself once received a Canada Council grant in visual art/photography just six months after receiving one in poetry. To be accountable to the "Canadian canon" allowed a much freer realm of influences, similar to the state of affairs in Solomonic Jerusalem. It also offered the poet the possibility of looking back upon the present as if it were the past, while remaining firmly planted in the present—a present to which being "Canadian," in its marginality, might be the appropriate prophetic stance.

The population of Sumer, Akkad and the other provinces of third and early second millennium BCE southern Mesopotamia was roughly that of the province of British Columbia, where bpNichol was born. The Sumerian poet BP's readership was further constrained by the fact that only twenty percent of the population was literate. Of these, less than two percent could read historical tablets, since the majority up until this time (all this would change thanks to BP) used reading and writing for commercial and civil transactions.

Tablets of new "historical" documents were incised in editions of 50, at most, and distributed among the libraries of the known civilized world (again, somewhat less than the population of

Canada). By way of comparison, most of bpNichol's small press editions of his work (and all of them were small press because bp insisted upon it) averaged perhaps 500 copies, of which maybe 50 made their way to America or Britain. It was quite significant to bp that, aside from resisting the smothering mainstream, he be able to embody the perception that we have come virtually nowhere since the court poets at Ur and our repressed ur-text.

Let me repeat what history teaches. History teaches. With that epigraph (slightly altered) from Stein, *The Martyrology* begins.

DAY SEVEN.

> "the strange hill rose conical out of the farmer's field
> into the middle distance of the earth
> patterns are not apparent
>
> now i could make my home there
> set roots among the signs our fathers left
> one final music to be written
> long & beautiful a mourning for the worlds we lost"
>
> —*The Martyrology*, Book Two

1   The first six books of *The Martyrology* are now available anywhere in the world, to view or print out in their entirety, at the Coach House website, www.chbooks.com.

2   Armand Schwerner wrote *The Tablets*, which begins as a parody of academic Assyriology and ends as a notable American epic with only passing interest in historical Sumer.

THE FUTURE OF VISIONARY POETRY

This essay was first delivered as a lecture/reading on March 15, 2001 in New York City. Following the publication of my book, Dreams of Being Eaten Alive: The Literary Core of the Kabbalah, *I was asked to give the annual lecture on Mysticism for the Reform movement. It was held in the Park Avenue auditorium of Temple Emanu-El, where I had previously lectured on the Garden of Eden as an ironic biblical poem some twenty-odd years earlier, prior to any study of the Kabbalah.*

I counted several faces in the audience from that earlier occasion. In the intervening years we had all grown less complicated, it seemed to me, while the surrounding environment—city and country—had hardened into our simple frame, all of it set on the wall of a prehistorical past that was now more compelling than anything on it. I sensed it was urgent to feel our way across this wall and to open the window on the moment of our birth as a species. Not our individual births into human culture but our repressed species memory of first looking into the parental faces of a prior species. Certainly this is where our dense myth of Eden is rooted in the natural world.

Few people in the audience seemed to have thought these thoughts before. There is so much to do in New York, so many people to meet; it is easy to forget it is all taking place in a dark hive of cement and glass. Most came to hear something new but not too unfamiliar, and some of the sentences in the previous paragraph might have struck an appropriate mystical chord. If disorientation was necessary, however, I wanted the clarity and precision of visible nature to be the scaffold.

I realize that even in a Reform Jewish congregation, evolution may be liberally referred to, but is not generally addressed with care. For that reason, I have to apologize in advance because I will be discussing evolution in a certain detail that may not be as familiar as the Garden of Eden story. I can't help but feel that evolutionary theory should be known as publicly as the Bible. Words like "evolution" and "ecosystem" are battered and abused daily as metaphors in our popular culture. For instance, a new product (an eyeliner or a jetliner) may "evolve," or a new idea has "evolved"—when products and ideas are not at all germane to evolutionary theory, or to wild ecosystems.

The worst case I can relate is this: books and articles every day imagine that we can evolve in our heads, in our minds, rather than in our bodies. The only "evolution" to which I will be referring is the natural evolution of species in their—or our—bodies.

A footnote, now, in advance. It is a common occurrence in the media that habitat is confused with ecosystem. A habitat refers to a natural area in which one species is central, surrounded by what it needs to survive, its habitat. An ecosystem is far away from that and as close relatively to a kabbalistic system as anything I have encountered. In an ecosystem, the center is invisible, and what you actually see is the representation of invisible relationships in time and space between thousands of species in the air, under ground, in the animals and plants and even in the stomachs of the animals and in the trunks of the trees. In addition to those thousands there are additional thousands of species in any particular wild ecosystem that have already become extinct, and those extinct species, from microbes to larger animals, were also important to making up that ecosystem. No one has ever found the center of an ecosystem nor are they ever likely to.

One bibliographic note in advance as well: I refer to my book, *The Eden Revelation*, which is not yet finished. However, there's another I'd recommend to you tonight because it's already in print, *The Ecology of Eden*. The author, Evan Eisenberg, has a composer's ear for the intangible orchestration of evolution.

Now, a little envoi from Chaim Nachman Bialik, the elemental Jewish modernist poet: "Real art, which is not a means to a livelihood….real art, like the Torah, cannot be truly served except by him who sacrifices his life for it—in order to give life. What matters is the vital relation of the artist to the form of life that lies before him. If an artist disqualifies any form of life as unsuitable for art, the question at once arises whether it is not he himself who is unqualified in that particular regard."

Written in 1916, taken from an essay about the Talmud (in *Revealment and Concealment*, 2000), this excerpt is part of a radical argument for the secular significance of *Halachah*, or religious law, over *Aggadah*, the more obviously secular literature of legends and stories. Almost a century later, it is clear Bialik interpreted the *Mishnah*, the codification of the law in the Talmud, by putting the law aside and reading the background anxiety for how to live in the natural world. A modernist concern about preserving the spirit of the Talmud suddenly matches our contemporary need to preserve our natural world itself. This need grounds my subject tonight, visionary poetry, in a form of life that the literary world still finds unsuitable, namely restoration ecology.

During the past year I've been living in Berkeley, California, and like the entire San Francisco Bay Area it is built up. Ninety-five percent of the wild ecosystems have been destroyed. Those coming from the more pristine northern California town of Eureka refer to the "eyesore of the Bay," yet most people I meet consider the Bay Area to have "beautiful views." Even environmentalists, who speak of "saving what is left," are rarely understood to be mourning an ecosystem that has been lost. But what is left is beautiful in the way a cemetery or garden often is: a pacified, domesticated nature, reduced to human scale and impoverished by being made in our image.

I start with where I live for this reason: Over a decade ago, I left Manhattan to live near the Florida Everglades and work with tropical biologists on ecosystem restoration. At the same time, I continued my practices of poetry, prose poetry and translation, in particular of Kabbalistic literature, because I had made a personally rewarding discovery: the science of natural restoration and the restoration of the Garden of Eden, the latter a key conceptual device of Kabbalistic authors—both of these restorations take place at frontiers that few people know about.

When you think of Miami, as I once did in my Northeast Corridor ignorance, you probably imagine B-movie vice, Latin and beach fashions, or a place where parents might retire; a balmy place but hardly one that is exotic. Yet in areas bordering Miami, an exotic frontier outclasses even anything in the Caribbean islands, although 90% of the local residents are in willful ignorance of the native ecosystem (a tad higher percentage of people than those in denial over the ecosystem degradation of San Francisco).

For most of the '90s, I lived half an hour from Everglades National Park, and only three minutes from a preserved remnant of Mangrove forest and tropical Hammock, which is the word for a hardwood island in a freshwater wetland. This remnant of the Everglades was invisible to most. Imagine returning to Lithuania to visit your family's ancestral town and finding nothing familiar there, nothing of the landmarks you'd heard about in stories. Not even finding the graveyard. That's what most people experience today in the Everglades ecosystem.

In order to see it, what's required is a desire to read the invisible: what had once flourished there and was then ripped out and covered over, a blind project of the twentieth century. I first had that experience in the 1960s, when I went to visit my father's town in the former Czechoslovakia. It seemed like a ghost town. Only a remnant of Gypsies reminded me of my father's stories, yet the Roma people I saw were sullen and discriminated against, hardly the vibrant community where my father learned to play gypsy fiddle.

The key to describing a healthy ecosystem is the word invisible. Ecosystem is actually a play on the word system because even if there were a center to it, it is now lost in time and space. Our bodies are a much simpler version of a similar system. Once upon a time, the heart or the brain was thought of as its center, but we know how silly that sounds now. Even with a complicated evolutionary answer, however, we are simply one species among a vast interdependency both within our bodies and without. But because we still consider our human bodies to have transcended their original ecosystem, whether spiritually or culturally, the questions we ask about ourselves remain essentially the same as they were for Kabbalists at the beginning of the Second Millenium. As well, for too many of us human consciousness as represented by a human soul still smacks of the supernatural, instead of having found natural analogues.

The great Kabbalists of the Middle Ages made the body the central metaphor of human transcendence. And at the center of this male body was the phallus, since reproduction was the proof and reward for transcending death. For the Kabbalists, the human body stood in for the mystery of a divine body, in whose image Adam was created. Yet this is not the Adam who left the Garden of Eden with Eve to become our father. Rather, it is the primordial Adam, *Adam*

Kadmon—with his phallus intact, so to speak—and his Garden is a wild ecosystem unlike any domesticated garden we know. The Kabbalistic Garden of Eden could be said to be as unknown and invisible as our original ecosystem—and not merely the one in which Homo sapiens evolved but the one in which the next species in the Homo line will evolve as well. There is a part of us that can recognize this invisible Garden, a part we may call the invisible soul. No matter how it sits in us, it is always outside of our conscious and unconscious cultures of knowledge.

To go outside of our common culture, immerse yourself for a moment in the Kabbalah. In this brief passage from *Dreams of Being Eaten Alive*, Samael and Lilith each represent the satanic "other side" of civilization—a side out<u>side</u>.

Now return: Adam and Eve are still in Paradise when Samael, with a little boy in tow, accosts Eve. "Would you mind merely keeping an eye on my son?" he asks her. "I will soon return." Eve agrees.

Returning from a walk in Paradise, Adam follows the piercing squeals of the child back to Eve.

"It is Samael's," she tells a vexed Adam. His anxiety increases along with the screams of the little one, which grow unbearably violent. Beside himself, Adam delivers a blow that kills the youngster then and there. Yet its body continues to wail at a fever pitch, monstrous groans that do not stop when Adam cuts the corpse into bits.

Then Adam cooked the pieces of flesh and bone that remained, to wipe out this fiend. Together with Eve, he ate all that was left. They had hardly finished when Samael called for his son. Denying any knowledge of his son, the culprits were protesting their innocence when suddenly a louder voice cried out from within their stomachs to silence them: it was the dead boy's voice, come straight from their hearts, his words directed to Samael.

"Leave me, now that I've pierced the hearts of both Adam and Eve. I remain in their hearts forever, and in their children's hearts, their children's children—until the last generation I abide there."

Not long ago, simply the word tropic suggested a place outside of civilization. We had quaint words like "jungle" to suggest it, although we now realize that what we had called the Amazon jungle is in fact the richest and most complex ecosystem. In the same way, the complexity of the body has deepened into the mystery of biodiversity. The millions of species among which we are every day discovering our relationship bespeak a beauty and knowledge—a poetry—not yet known to us.

Stop for a moment to consider this visionary poetry of the future. It is not poetry that is preferred today, the kind that "so wonderfully explains us and our time to ourselves." I lift this phrase from the New York Times Book Review a few weeks ago, when it was used to describe the late poet James Merrill's *Collected Poems*.

A visionary poetry, on the other hand, instead of omnisciently embodying the present, must see *through* its omniscience to explore the future. We knew this type of exploring in early childhood, in a pre-linguistic innocence. Instead of illuminating the mind, it must insist on the body and only the body. And yet this body of the sexually inquisitive child is an object of great unknowing. As the child transforms its sexuality into *the search for* sexuality—where do babies come from? or later, where do words come from?—it is not long before he or she ends in failure. We are in a similar search today, in the context of frontier ecosystem science. The system eludes us, and the ecosystem appears to us as if a body we are immersed in. As I would re-emphasize, it is a body that is familiar to both Kabbalist and visionary poet.

To disarm the adult version of a child's grandiosity, both Kabbalist and visionary poet begin their approach to the future in the disguise of failure. A new work must always appear to be a lost book from the past, or a translation of a lost book, or the story and words of a lost poet or prophet, such as Moses in the Five Books of Moses, Jesus in the Gospels, or Rav

Shimon bar Yohai in the Kabbalah's Zohar. DeLeon, the author of the Zohar, posed as editor and commentator rather than as writer of his text.

If a poetic text claims to be either new or directly inspired, it is suspect as visionary poetry. It is a hard reality to embrace for a poet, because it means one must live one's life in disguise as something lesser: a mere translator, for instance.

If I were to be reading to you now from my own poetry I would be an imposter, but how would you know it? Because far from having the lost or disarmed mind required of a Kabbalist—"lost" in the sense of outside conventional civilization—I would be seen to be attempting to mount my work, to frame it, to throw a spotlight on it, or to do whatever it takes to stand on a stage somewhere and receive a prize and listen to others extoll the virtues of the mind one is presumed to have in one's possession.

In disguise, however, it is my pleasure and purpose to be able to conduct the search, on your behalf, for what is missing or invisible in our constricted idea of what passes for civilization today. What passes for the present moment.

Can one imagine Moses DeLeon, author of the *Zohar*, on a stage receiving a prize for this masterwork of Kabbalah? The thought is ludicrous. Yes, Isaac Bashevis Singer accepted the Nobel Prize. But if you look closely at his Nobel Speech, you will see that he is admitting he has sent an imposter to stand in for the ghosts of the other great Yiddish poets and writers who were gassed in Europe. Tellingly, he asserts that the ghost language in which he writes nevertheless has a future.

When disasters of human making occur—wars and genocide—it is the visionary poet who reminds us that we are a limited species, and that it is hopeful to look toward a more natural future rather than simply a narrow human future and its supernatural wishes. A parallel description of our visionary future (taken from a book-in-progress I will discuss shortly) might sound like this:

from A New Religion

A new possibility for studying the soul exists because we can now conceive of an afterlife in the form of an unexplored ecosystem. Suddenly, we have an advanced conceptual framework in which other species represent what we used to think of as spirit, or angels and demons. The key to this afterlife is that it be beyond the human, for there's little nourishment in imagining simply a human future anymore. Here is the point at which a soul-starved secular culture can meet a reality-starved religious history.

Since this meeting has not yet occurred, our secular arts continue to project the angst and poignancy of circumscribed lives. Far from being able to persuade, science represses spiritual uncertainty (where do our souls reside?) while religion avoids the teaching of evolutionary origins. The discovery that this book will propose begins with the gene-altered mouse. Imagine that the mouse has become more intelligent by desiring to explore and by being able to tap into its drive to evolve. This discovery appears counter-intuitive, since evolving is a kind of getting lost and disappearing into the very thing we fear and are trying to manage with our intelligence: nature itself. Instead of merely changing the way we see the world, we must come to "see" and feel evolution as more central to our lives than human culture. *The species of Homo sapiens will have to be left behind.* It will become a species we love and have dear feelings about, but it will no longer be us.

Evolution teaches that things of the past never simply go away. Homo sapiens will be alive in us but we'll be another species. What will that be? Any answer will only disappoint, because each of us must experience that gene-altered feeling of disappearance on his or her own.

Some of you may feel lost in the picture of the future I am painting. In this, however, you are not unlike a mystic—who I've represented as a Kabbalist, a visionary poet, or a frontier scientist. Mysticism shares with visionary poetry a tolerance for the irrational but not for incoherence. Lost, one's coherence is found in the search for a future that can embody the loss. What might that coherence or visionary poetics be today? I believe it can be found in a love for the invisible.

A "habitat" can be made visible because any one species' needs are at the center of it, but the invisible ecosystem is a visionary imagining of relationships over evolutionary time and space. It can only be "seen" in the creative process of re-imagining the future. Its opposite is what we call the environment; that is, whatever is visible around us, however despoiled it may be and however lazy our response. It tells us where we are and that is all.

Imagining the future in mysticism often leads briskly to the supernatural and for that reason there is a constant struggle among its visionaries to make it a science. The Kabbalah was considered a science among its authors. As a system of reading, it synthesized adult experience with the lost clarity of pre-linguistic childhood. The innocence of childhood omniscience is something I described earlier as a "return to the Garden of Eden"—and to the belief that one could communicate with the unknown without it having to be fully understood. A visionary poet, by "finding" a lost past, embodies this omniscience in a language and form that must seem familiar and disorienting at the same time.

In religion, in science, and in art, one thing that is now converging is a desire to evolve. That is, a desire in each discipline to see ourselves from outside. Through a Kabbalist lens, it would look like a return to the Garden of Eden by evolving into a new Homo species—thereby, to look back poignantly from outside human civilization.

Tracking this desire to evolve, for the past several years I have collaborated on a new work, *The Eden Revelation*, with my scientist wife, Dr. Rhonda Rosenberg. Our focus has been to bring not only knowledge to bear on the future, but poetry as well. Imagine talking about mysticism but not experiencing it; imagine talking about classic Blues but never experiencing it, never having been immersed. Imagine describing a dream without ever having had one. In the same way, it makes little sense to envision a creative ecosystem—one healthy enough for new species to evolve—without stepping into it.

In fact, we have all been there but few of us have known it. *The Eden Revelation* translates this experience into a work that takes the form of both novel and essay.

Like the passage offered a moment ago from "A New Religion," the one that follows, about Eden, is from the "essay" side of *The Eden Revelation*:

from A New Model of Disappearance

Some literary critics have found in the Genesis story an anxious longing for something that never was or never can be again. But what if we found proof that the Garden really existed, albeit in another form? What if the Genesis story is the shadow memory of what we are beginning to discover through the restoring of endangered ecosystems around the world? Origins would have to be felt; evolution would have to be experienced by us in our deepest emotions.

The Eden Revelation reflects this experience. The disappearance of Adam and Eve from Eden turns into a flight—a fleeing into a panic, yes, but also into a sweet mutability that is felt and experienced as the first bite of an apple, a seductive fruit offered by a cunning plant. The plant is seeking to reproduce and also to explore new terrain for itself, and so some of its seeds may be mutations that can thrive in foreign soil. We all contain genetic mutations. In a sense, we are half-evolved already. To become the true explorers we were created to be, we must also learn to let go of our exclusive humanity. Here is the way it was represented in Hebraic tradition, before Genesis had been composed, in an excerpt from one of the lost books I have restored and translated, *The Lost Book of Paradise.*

> Adam:
> Take this palm that ravishes me, uncoiling
> An articulate head, wild
> Like a scholar's, she speaks
> Directly to my thoughts, bypassing sound—
> As light outlines a tree, colors and shapes it
> So words do thought
> Leaves each a feather of a finger
> Pleated into a fan…

What is crucial to notice here is that neither Adam nor Eve are portrayed as special creations; instead, the palm tree in this passage is an equal species. Elements of this awareness survive in the Genesis story, as Adam names the other species in a process of exploration. In the earlier Garden story, exploration is shown to be not just a human endeavor but natural to all wild species. When trees explore the soil or track the light, they are also searching out new territory to colonize or a new ecosystem in which to evolve.

Now, if the Garden were an ecosystem, we would expect that the story of Adam and Eve would go like this:

> Some of the Homo species were exploring the edges of Eden and they were drawn further toward trees that resembled one in the middle of the Garden. So pleased were they with the taste of

its fruit that they went on further than ever before.

One couple was cut off, however, by rising water they could not return across. As Adam and Eve looked for another way home, they wandered further from Eden and they began to be frightened. No longer did they find the indescribable fruits from the trees of Eden to which they were accustomed. Now they had to forage and dig for tubers; the weather was fierce and water was harder to find; wild animals began to threaten them.

Finally, Adam and Eve were in a panic: instead of finding an alternate route back to Eden, they had become permanently lost outside of it. They had, in effect, disappeared from Eden. The ecosystems they entered were increasingly desert-like and they feared for their lives.

Then, one day, they stumbled into a desert oasis that reminded them of Eden. It was merely a remnant, a tiny pocket of Eden, but here they would live out their days, while their children and grandchildren moved on and adapted to the new ecosystems surrounding them, learning to hunt and gather, and even to build cities....

In the story created above, myth and evolution converge, but neither art nor science could move us if the context of the disappearance of Eden was not established. Ancient scholars were not afraid to be poets. In the great culture of ancient Israel, it was the poets who served as analysts of myths, drawing upon the biologists, botanists, and scholars of their day, tenders of the fields and palace archives. Nature was not to be simply dominated but lived beside and tended; the active verb, *l'shamrah* (to tend, in early Hebraic usage), survives prominently in Genesis.

On the poetic side of *The Eden Revelation*, consider a passage from another lost book, "The Scroll of the History of Adam." I have restored and translated several fragments from this early Hebraic epic.

Adam Speaks

To be an observer—it's almost as if I wasn't here. Then who am I? Nothing looks back at me, as everything did in Eden, not unless I stir it. All the animals are small and hiding but when the squirrel comes up to me he turns and runs as I reach out my hand. He too was alone and thought I was a bush until I moved.

But then I saw a tree in the water, wavering. What kind of wind stirs it so, I thought, and then saw it was a reflection of a tree on the bank. I looked up to the bank, saw many trees of differing size and shape but not one resembling the water reflection. I was scared for a moment, why?

In that moment the imagined tree in the water had a life of its own—beyond my conscious thought. That was me, then, me in the landscape, existing outside myself; I could not possess that thought and there it was; I could not name that tree, as I named all I faced in Eden.

Later, when it was dark, I thought of all this and realized that the tree in water was dark, a dark blue, taking on the water's color. On the bank, the trees with their leaves were a light green, made lighter by the light coming through. In the water, the light played on the surface and made the tree a dense shape, the leaves letting no light through. So when I looked to the shore I was tricked by the light into seeing different shapes. My memory holds the images true, so that I may find the trick. And now, even in the dark, my memory holds the moment, and I am more alone again; before, tricked by changing light, in my fear I found another presence sharing my vision, a presence there before me, like a mother. I was happy then, for a moment, transformed in time.

Later, finding the trick, I knew that I would always have to learn what I didn't know, venturing out alone. I would make the mistakes made in Eden, over and over again. I mistook the tree in water for a god, a presence not of my world—the mother I never had. Was she there, nonetheless, hidden deeper under things than it appears?

I have to think so; and when I don't, my loneliness crawls inside my skin, turning it into a cold, rough hide.

We have just watched Adam in the act of losing himself but then finding he is still there; it was his sense of omniscience that was lost, leaving him to search among the plants and animals for his place. For contemporary parallels, turn again to the essay-side of the book, to the tangibility of our displacement from nature and the loss of our tails—what might be called an unconscious spiritual dread of the future.

The Invisible and the Tail-less

Inevitably we run up against the counter-intuitive, the invisible part of nature. Sustainability is a paradigm that works with the visible and with common sense. Yet the plants and animals we can see are expressions of an ecosystem, not the ecosystem itself. Our soul knows that the most significant part of nature is invisible but our conscious mind does not. And what is our idea of a soul but the invisible counterpart within us? Since we can sense the non-sensible, we harbor more fear and avoidance of nature than the rest of the plant and animal kingdoms. Is that what makes us superior, after all—fear and avoidance? The nervous system of a tree or fish fears its predators and knows its defenses are limited, but its owner is quite at home in the ecosystem. Instead of fearing the invisible or what it does not know, a tree tracks the light, the water, and its neighbors around it. Individuals of each species explore the borders of their ecosystem for a new niche in which to evolve.

Tail-less, humans have had to connect to the invisible parts of their world through culture, the rough tales of the unknown. We exist almost exclusively within our cultures, largely cut off from the original ecosystem in which we evolved. We could be writing this essay in a jail cell, if we had to. Most other living things stay in touch with their ecosystems and gain intelligence from this, releasing them from need of a bigger brain. They are in touch with their ecosystem by means of an antenna-like appendage that may often appear as a tail. We are beginning to learn that perhaps tails are as valuable as brains in the realm of intelligence.

Sustainability, like so many of our visions of the world, is a big-brain strategy for survival. We remain unmoved, continuing to scan the cultural landscape for something that corresponds to a condition in ourselves that has awakened to painful feelings about the future. Is it the "faith-based communities" that some political candidates speak of? Or, can "common sense" alone ease our minds?

Although we are relatively free as we write this, on a verandah at the edge of the wild Everglades, we have to admit that not even visions of the future work anymore. Instead of vision and imagination we have spiritual dread of the story of bodily evolution on the inspirational level; and on the intellectual level, scientific resistance to the inspired creation stories of religion. That is, to what future does evolutionary theory inspire us? And what kind of future can be intellectually grounded in the Garden of Eden? For too many, there is no story but that of the bottom-line: human development.

The mis-characterization of evolution as forms of progress and survival continues to circulate. We would be wrong to listen, because the story of evolution is about the creation of the soul—a soul that science, religion and art can each admit represents the unknown about consciousness. Part metaphysics, part metaphor, and now undeniably palpable, the future of evolution could become a soul-sustaining tale for the tail-less.

In order to explore an entrance into the future we must follow the tale of evolutionary disembodiment, all that is left of our real tail. In a passage of monologue from a fictional character in *The Eden Revelation*—Archibald Shechner, an Israeli archaeologist who has lost his mind, and heard a voice in his head—disorientation becomes exploration. It is a voice placed there by the ecosystem, representing the instinctual communication between an organism and the ecosystem that "unknowingly" conceived and nurtured it.

TELESCOPE AND PENISFISH

Shape of thought is entirely sexual, I realize. Exploration is a form of foreplay; problem-solving resembles intercourse. What do we think about? Mostly other people or bodies; our own body. Watched my cat explore the yard like a scientist but when another cat shows up he loses interest in anything else. Walk down a street and think about clothes for instance, on a person or in a window; culture and the known. The unknown: someone else's thinking, even in a book. Or where things come from. Parrots in their cages in the zoo have little labels affixed as to country of origin. They do not come from countries! Impossible to think about where they really come from, forests that evolved them. Impossible to ask new questions without considering the ecosystem; the same's true for us. All that's left of our original ecosystem is simply an extension of our sex lives, wherever we live it. A couple could have a child in a space capsule, like parrots in cages. Or in a city or on a farm—makes no difference, its all cages now, separated from the ecosystem that shaped us. All that's left that's original is sex.

Good God, could I ever let anyone read this? Society resists fear of the unknown but these thoughts are scary. Caught a small penisfish in a dream, bright orange with blue markings, it jumped into my hands. I was reading the transcripts which Betti had bound like a book. Suddenly the fish hopped onto the book in my lap, just as I was admiring its beauty, and as I flinched, the opened book slid between my legs, sandwiching the fish. Before I could think I snapped my legs closed to catch the falling book. All the while I'd worried for the fish's safety out of water: it seemed to breathe and be quite alright, but how could that be? Wondered at its beauty but at the same time felt close to panic about getting it back into water.

The closed book slid onto the floor. Dead, I thought first, and then: I would rather have its life than its beauty. The beauty remains in the book, an excitement, a problem solved, a closure. I would rather be running to the water, its home, with the living thing. Rather feel it alive than framed in mind: my minutely-wired mirror of an ecosystem.

A sexual story of desire and exploration. An erected telescope: the ancient heavens are still alive, all the way back to its origin! Within, genes are the living, interpretive telescope by which to read our own beginnings and—what is most deeply hidden in there—a drive to evolve. Look back at the sky and its infinite explosions and unfurling gaseous arms. How deeply buried the drive to spurt forth something entirely new! Our bodies are wired with a fearful nervous system, cautious of the unknown. Surely we will now explore a way to rewire a more daring body. Won't even passion drive us to it?

OF DAVID ROSENBERG'S books in the past decade, two have been New York Times Notable Books of the Year, while a third, *A Poet's Bible*, was given the PEN/Book-of-the-Month Club Prize, the first major literary award for a biblical translation. Rosenberg's *The Book of J*, with commentary by Harold Bloom, was a national bestseller. More recently, his 1973 volume, *The Necessity of Poetry*, was restored online (chbooks.com) and his book on the Kabbalah, *Dreams of Being Eaten Alive*, has been released in paperback. Residing near the Everglades with his wife, the writer Rhonda Rosenberg, they are completing their multi-genred opus of the '90s, *The Eden Revelation: The Converging Desire to Evolve in Science, Religion and Art*.

Printed by Amazon Italia Logistica S.r.l.
Torrazza Piemonte (TO), Italy